second edition

rudiments
of
MUSIC

Robert W. Ottman
Frank D. Mainous
School of Music, North Texas State University

Prentice-Hall, Inc., Englewood Cliffs, New Jersey 07632

Library of Congress Cataloging-in-Publication Data

OTTMAN, ROBERT W.
    Rudiments of music.

    Includes index.
    1. Music—Theory, Elementary.
I. Mainous,Frank D. II. Title.
MT7.O82 1987   781   86-22626
ISBN 0-13-783671-6

Editorial/production supervision and
    interior design: Arthur Maisel
Manufacturing buyer: Ray Keating
Page layout: Peggy Finnerty

Robert W. Ottman, MUSIC FOR SIGHT SINGING, c 1967, pp. 22, 27, 28,
29, 30, 32, 33, 125, 126.   Reprinted by permission of Prentice-Hall, Inc.,
Englewood Cliffs, New Jersey.
Robert W. Ottman/Frank D. Mainous, PROGRAMMED RUDIMENTS OF
MUSIC, c 1979, pp. 176, 180, 333, 335, 337, 338, 340. Reprinted by per-
mission of Prentice-Hall, Inc., Englewood Cliffs, New Jersey.

Printed in the United States of America

10   9   8

0-13-783671-6   01

Prentice-Hall International (UK) Limited, *London*
Prentice-Hall of Australia Pty. Limited, *Sydney*
Prentice-Hall Canada Inc., *Toronto*
Prentice-Hall Hispanoamericana, S.A., *Mexico*
Prentice-Hall of India Private Limited, *New Delhi*
Prentice-Hall of Japan, Inc., *Tokyo*
Prentice-Hall of Southeast Asia Pte. Ltd., *Singapore*
Editora Prentice-Hall do Brasil, Ltda., *Rio de Janeiro*

Contents

FOOTHILL COLLEGE BOOKSTORE
(415) 949-7305

A SERVICE CHARGE WILL BE ASSESSED ON RETURNED CHECKS

PROTECT YOUR INVESTMENT
SAVE THIS RECEIPT ➡

NO RECEIPT — NO RETURNS
BEGINNING OF THE QUARTER RETURNS POLICY

A full refund will be given on new or used books IF ..... ➡

1. YOU PRESENT YOUR CASH REGISTER RECEIPT .
2. You DO NOT marr or write in your Books-Return New Books in brand new, clean condition.
3. Do not mark or write in your new book(s) until you receive instructor verification that it is the correct text(s) for your class.
4. Wrapped or boxed merchandise must not be unwrapped or opened.
5. You return books for fall, winter or spring by the END OF THE SECOND WEEK from the starting of that respective quarter.
6. Summer refund dates will be posted.
7. The Manager reserves the right to make the decision on the condition or saleability of the merchandise.

STANDARD RETURN POLICY
1. Same as above except you have ONLY 5 WORKING DAYS from the DATE ON YOUR RECEIPT.

refunds will be given on books during the last **five** weeks of any

KEEP YOUR RECEIPT

```
         FOOTHILL BOOKSTORE
        LAST DAY FOR REFUNDS
           APRIL 19, 1993

04/05/93                    11:25AM
003#1770                    **B
ANUPRIYA

TXT BOOK              T1$43.75
MDSE ST                 $43.75
TAX 1                    $3.61
***TOTAL                $47.36
CASH                    $50.00
CHANGE                   $2.64
```

SELL BACK POLICY

SELL YOUR NEW & USED BOOKS FOR CASH AT THE BOOKSTORE DURING FINALS WEEK. YOUR BOOKS MAY BE WORTH UP TO 50% — — RECEIPTS NOT NEEDED —

THE BOOKSTORE CANNOT GUARANTEE THE BUYBACK OF ANY BOOK AT ANYTIME.

Preface

Rudiments of Music is for beginners in music theory; the material covered is often known under such titles as "Elements of Music," "Basic Principles of Music," or "Music Fundamentals," and precedes more advanced theoretical studies such as Harmony, Counterpoint, and Orchestration. In this book, we will study music notation, pitch, the keyboard, time, scales, intervals, and elementary concepts of harmony. This revised edition presents a format designed to give the teacher/student various options in choosing the sequence of presentation. See "Suggestions for the Use of this Book" immediately following this Preface.

The basic principle behind each subject listed above (notation, pitch, etc.) is easy enough to understand. If that were all that is necessary, this book would be much smaller than it is. In fact, you can look up these topics in a music dictionary if you need only to know the principles involved. If, however, a study of these principles is to aid you in better performing ability, it is necessary that you be able to apply these principles quickly and accurately in a given musical situation. To this end, *Rudiments of Music* provides you with enough practice in each lesson that not only will you be able to say, "Yes, I've got the general idea," but more important, you can say, "I can actually do these things quickly and accurately." Then you will receive your dividends in the form of better understanding of the music you perform, and quicker learning and more accurate performance of your music. In addition, you will have laid the groundwork for more advanced theoretical courses—perhaps even for original composition—and for increased appreciation and enjoyment of all music.

Robert W. Ottman
Frank D. Mainous

Suggestions for the Use of this Book

Sequence of Chapters

After Chapters 1 and 2 (Pitch), the early chapters on *Time* and *Pitch* are found alternately, allowing various options for the use of this book. The following sequences of presentation are possible:

(1) Complete each chapter in the order of presentation in the book. *Pitch* and *Time* will be studied alternately in carefully calculated increments so that a two-pronged advancement can be satisfactorily maintained by the student.

(2) Continue a particular study for a few chapters (two or more) as desired. For example, upon completion of Chapter 2, *Pitch,* go immediately to Chapter 4, the next chapter on *Pitch*. To assist in this sequence of presentation, a reference at the end of each chapter indicates the next chapter number in that subject area. Ultimately, return to chapters skipped in other subject areas.

Or, continue a particular study for several chapters before working in other subject areas, a presentation similar to that above but with greater scope.

These are the chapter numbers in each subject area:

> *Pitch:* 1, 2, 4, 6, 8, 10, 13, 14
> (Chapters 15, 16, and 17 may also be deployed with *Pitch*)
> *Time:* 3, 5, 7, 9, 11, 12
> *Harmony:* 18–21

(3) Study both *Pitch* and *Time* in each class session. When combined for presentation, chapters can easily be halved, quartered, or otherwise abridged to fit class time. Exercises (discussed below) readily accommodate this plan of presentation.

Exercises

Each chapter presentation is followed by a group of appropriate exercises. Marginal references throughout the presentation direct the student to an exercise providing practice in the particular material just covered. Upon completion of each exercise (or group of exercises), a page reference directs the student back to the location in the book where the presentation continues. This procedure for instant application of exercises is recommended. Optionally, exercises can be deferred and worked as a group at the end of the chapter.

Harmony

New to this revised edition are Chapters 18–21 on the subject of *Harmony*. These chapters allow students to apply in a practical manner much of their acquired knowledge of the basics of music. The chapters are not intended to represent a complete presentation of the harmonic materials included, but they will conveniently serve as a transition or link to a formal course in the subject.

When classroom keyboard facilities are limited, Chapters 19 and 21 may be omitted. Chapters 18 and 20 may be studied in succession. They provide all the intended harmonic material, plus exercises in harmonic structures and harmonic analysis.

CHAPTER ONE

Pitch

Pitch
The Staff
The Musical Alphabet
Clefs, Treble and Bass
Ledger Lines
Uses of Treble and Bass Clefs
The Great Staff

Obviously the most important aspect of music is its *sound,* and all study of music should have as its primary goal the production of correct and meaningful sound. Essential to this goal is the study of symbols used to notate musical sound on paper. Sound consists of four elements: (1) pitch, (2) duration, (3) intensity, and (4) timbre. Our studies will be principally those related to pitch and duration (time),[1] beginning with the notation of *pitch.*

Pitch

When we hear two different sounds produced by a musical instrument such as the piano, we hear one of the sounds as being higher or lower than the other. Sounds, of course, are not "high" or "low" in the sense that they are different heights above ground level, but sounds do give a feeling of highness and lowness in relation to each other. This property of sound, its seeming highness or lowness, is called *pitch.* To indicate on paper the difference in pitch in musical sound, we use a device called the *staff.*

The Staff

The music *staff* (plural, *staves*) consists of five parallel horizontal lines and four resultant spaces. These lines and spaces represent successively higher pitches when progressing from the lowest to the highest line.

The lines are numbered from the bottom to the top, 1 through 5. Spaces are similarly numbered from the bottom, 1 through 4. The pitches represented by lines and spaces are identified by letters of the *musical alphabet.*

---

1. For discussion of intensity and timbre, see Appendix 1, *Elementary Acoustics.*

FIGURE 1.1 *The Staff.*

```
5th line----                                  ----4th space )
4th line----  _____  ----3rd space }   higher pitches
            { 3rd line----  _____  -----3rd space }
lower pitches{2nd line----  _____  --2nd space
            ( 1st line----                       -1st space
```

EXERCISE 1.1

The Musical Alphabet

The first seven letters of the alphabet, A B C D E F G, comprise the musical alphabet. These letters are used to name the lines and spaces of the staff, but the particular letter assigned to a specific line or space is determined by a symbol appearing at the beginning of the staff called a *clef*.

Clefs

The two clefs most commonly used in music are (1) 𝄞, the G clef, in which the lower loop encircles a line of the staff to be designated as G; and (2) 𝄢, the F clef, in which the two dots are found on either side of a line of the staff to be designated as F. When the G clef is placed on the staff in a certain position, it is called the *treble clef*.

Treble Clef

EXERCISE 1.2

When the G clef is placed on the staff with the lower loop encircling the second line it is known as the *treble clef*.

Thus the second line of the staff receives the designation G. By fixing G on the staff, the names of other lines and spaces are also determined. Letters of the musical alphabet are employed in order on ascending adjacent lines and spaces (staff degrees). After G, A follows on the next higher staff degree, which is the second space.

FIGURE 1.2 *Treble Clef and Names of the Lines and Spaces.*

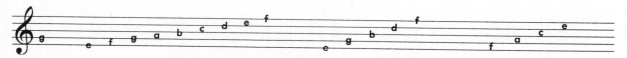

**EXERCISES
1.3, 1.4**

Lines and spaces receive different designations when the F clef is placed on the staff in a certain position and called the *bass clef*.

Bass Clef

EXERCISE 1.5

When the F clef is placed on the staff with the two dots on either side of the fourth line, it is known as the *bass clef*.

Thus the fourth line of the staff receives the designation F. By fixing F on the staff, the names of the other lines and spaces are also determined. After F, G follows on the next higher staff degree, which is the fourth space.

FIGURE 1.3 *Bass Clef and Names of the Lines and Spaces.*

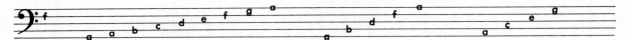

At times a musical sound may be either higher or lower than those pitches represented by lines and spaces of the staff. Means of writing such pitches are provided by *ledger lines.*

EXERCISES
1.6, 1.7

Ledger Lines

Short lines added above and below the staff are called *ledger (leger) lines.* By extending the staff, ledger lines provide a means for indicating pitches either higher or lower than the limits of the five-line staff. Added ledger lines and resultant ledger spaces are drawn *equidistant* to lines and spaces of the staff. In Figure 1.4, notes[2] are used to show specific pitches more clearly.

FIGURE 1.4 *Ledger Lines.*

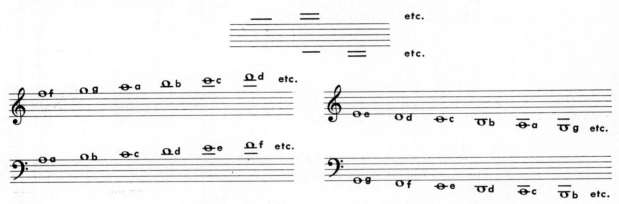

EXERCISES
1.8, 1.9, 1.10

Observe that a note on the space above or the space below the staff does *not* require a ledger line:

Uses of Treble and Bass Clefs

Players of instruments that produce relatively high pitches, such as flute, violin, and clarinet, read music written in the treble clef; players of instruments that produce relatively low pitches, such as trombone, tuba, and string bass, read music written in the bass clef. Soprano and alto voices use the treble clef. Tenor and bass voices use the bass clef. But when a staff accommodates only a

2. A note is a symbol based on an oval shape called a *note-head* (○, ●) to which may be added stems (e.g., ♩) and flags (e.g., ♪) in varying combinations to express pitch and duration of sound. The varieties of notes will be studied in Chapter 3.

Actually, only notes, which are named, should represent pitches; lines and spaces are merely numbered. However, in the absence of notes as in Figures 1.2 and 1.3, lines and spaces may be named just as though notes were present.

tenor voice the treble clef is used, with the understanding that the notation will be performed one octave (eight staff degrees) lower. (Explanation of *octave* will be found in Chapter 2). This procedure reduces the number of ledger lines needed. The variant clef signs, 𝄞 and 𝄞𝄞, serve the same purpose.

Music for the piano, which encompasses a wide range of pitches requires two staves in a combination called the *great staff.*

The Great Staff (Grand Staff)

When two staves are used together and are joined by a vertical line and a bracket, called a *brace,* this combination is known as the *great staff,* or *grand staff,* or *piano staff.*

In theory, the great staff is one large staff of eleven lines (Fig. 1.5*a*). The middle line is omitted (Fig. 1.5*b*) to create a separation, which permits quick visual discrimination of the upper and lower staff degrees.

FIGURE 1.5 *Eleven-line Staff.*

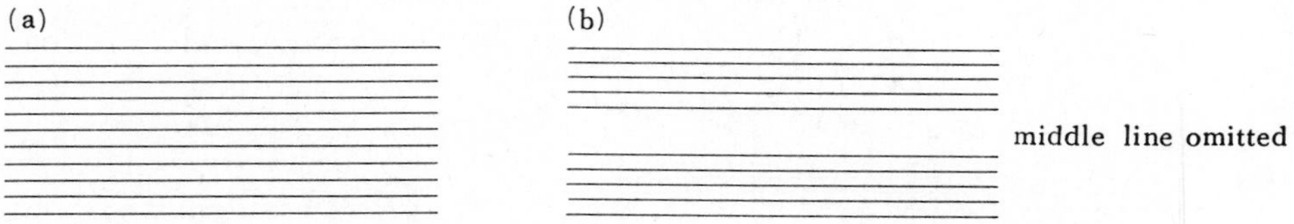

(a)

(b)

middle line omitted

With the brace added, the great staff is normally found with the treble clef in position on the upper five lines and the bass clef in position on the lower five lines.

FIGURE 1.6 *The Great Staff.*

If a ledger line were placed between the staves, like the omitted middle line in the eleven-line staff, then this single ledger line would be considered either the first ledger line above the bass or the first ledger line below the treble. See Figure 1.7 in which the pitch found on this ledger line centered between the staves is called *middle C.*

Notice that the space formed between the fifth bass line and the ledger line for middle C is occupied by the pitch B; continuing upward, notice that the space formed between the ledger line for middle C and the first treble line is occupied by the pitch D. Observe the alphabetical order of pitches on successive lines and spaces, from the bass upward through middle C and into the treble.

Figure 1.7, with the staves placed closely together to show relation of bass to treble, is purposefully a theoretical illustration. Actually, in printed music the

FIGURE 1.7 *Pitches on the Great Staff.*

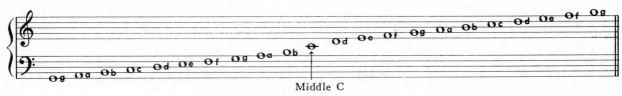

Middle C

distance between the two staves of the great staff is increased to provide sufficient room for several additional ledger lines both above the bass and below the treble. Figure 1.8 shows such a great staff. The series of pitches in the treble clef is identical in sound to the series in the bass clef; this is easily seen by comparing *middle C* in each clef.

FIGURE 1.8 *The Great Staff with Ledger Lines Above Bass and Below Treble.*

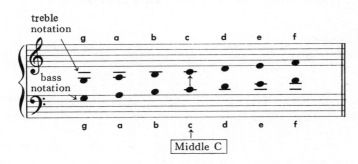

treble notation

bass notation

Middle C

EXERCISES 1.11, 1.12, 1.13

Remember that in printed music, or when you draw the great staff, the two staves are not close together but are well separated as in Figure 1.8 and as in the following music excerpts.

FIGURE 1.9 *The Great Staff: Usual Form.*

Beethoven, Sonata for Piano, Op. 2 No. 1[3]

Allegro

When necessary, each staff of the great staff may carry: (1) a treble clef (Fig. 1.10), (2) a bass clef (Fig. 1.11), or (3) a change from bass to treble, or vice versa (Fig. 1.12).

---

3. Opus (Latin, work) abbreviated op., together with a number identifies a composition, and is usually supplied by the composer.

5

FIGURE 1.10 *Great Staff: Two Treble Clefs.*

Mozart, Sonata for Piano, K.279[4]

FIGURE 1.11 *Great Staff: Two Bass Clefs.*

Chopin, Prelude, Op. 28, No. 20

FIGURE 1.12 *Great Staff with Change of Clef.*

Mozart, Sonata for Piano, K. 576

4. K., abbreviation for Ludwig von Köchel, who in 1862 made a chronological listing of Mozart's works. Mozart did not give his works opus numbers.

EXERCISE 1.1

The staff

Draw a staff to the right of the printed staff below:

(draw staff here)

Number the lines and spaces on the staff you drew. The bottom line is the first line.

(Upon completion of this exercise, *return* to page 2)

EXERCISE 1.2

Treble clef sign

On the staff below draw additional treble clef signs for practice. Be sure to make the lower loop encircle the second line of the staff.

(*Return* to page 2)

EXERCISE 1.3

Treble clef, lines and spaces

On staff *a*) draw a treble clef sign and on each line write the correct letter name. On staff *b*) draw a treble clef sign and on each space write the correct letter name.

a) treble clef, names of lines   *b*) treble clef, names of spaces

EXERCISE 1.4

Pitches on the staff, treble clef

Next to each note, write the letter name of the pitch.

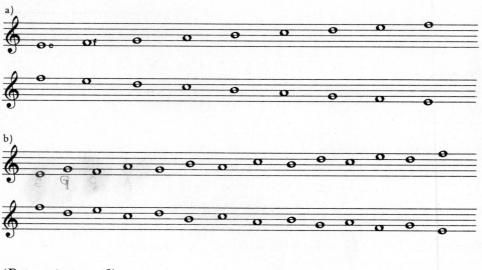

a)

b)

(*Return* to page 2)

EXERCISE 1.5

Bass clef sign

On the staff below draw additional bass clef signs for practice. Be sure to place the dots on either side of the fourth line of the staff.

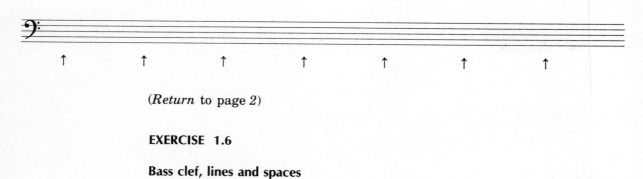

(*Return* to page 2)

EXERCISE 1.6

Bass clef, lines and spaces

On staff *a*) draw a bass clef sign and on each line write the correct letter name. On staff *b*) draw a bass clef sign and on each space write the correct letter name.

    a) bass clef, names of lines   *b*) bass clef, names of spaces

EXERCISE 1.7

Pitches on the staff, bass clef

Next to each note, write the letter name of the pitch.

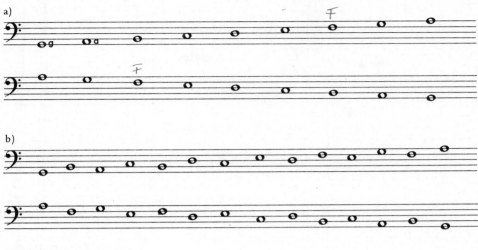

(*Return* to page *3*)

EXERCISE 1.8

Treble clef, ledger lines

On staff *a*) draw a treble clef sign. Name the pitches of the notes on the ledger lines and spaces above the staff. On staff *b*) draw a treble clef sign and name the pitches of the notes on the ledger lines and spaces below the staff.

a) treble clef, notes above staff

b) treble clef, notes below staff

EXERCISE 1.9

Bass clef, ledger lines

On staff *a*) draw a bass clef sign. Name the pitches of the notes on the ledger lines and spaces above the staff. On staff *b*) draw a bass clef sign and name the pitches of the notes on the ledger lines and spaces below the staff.

a) bass clef, notes above staff

b) bass clef, notes below staff

9

EXERCISE 1.10

Pitches above and below staff

Next to each note, write the letter name of the pitch:

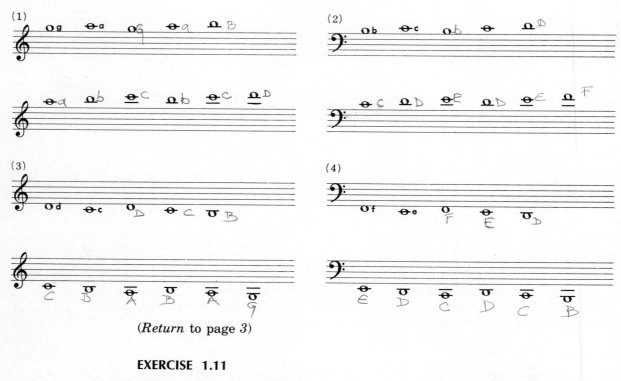

(*Return* to page 3)

EXERCISE 1.11

Pitches on the great staff

Next to each note, write the letter name of the pitch:

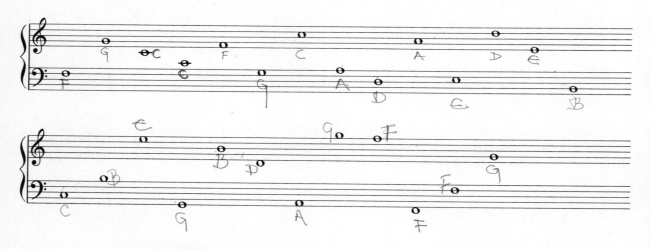

EXERCISE 1.12

Pitches in melody

The examples in this exercise are actual music examples and as such, they contain notation not yet studied. At this time we are interested only in naming the line or space on which the note-head $\circ$ or $\bullet$ is located (review footnote 2).[5]

Next to each note, write the letter name of the pitch.

(1) *America*

(2) *Auld Lang Syne*

(3) MSS 105[6]

(4) MSS 97

5. Examples of actual music will be used throughout the text and at times will contain elements not yet studied. These examples have been chosen to illustrate most efficiently the element under study; the remaining elements will not be found essential to the particular study, and they will be covered in later chapters.

6. MSS: *Music for Sight Singing* (third edition) by Robert W. Ottman, Prentice-Hall, Inc., 1986.

EXERCISE 1.13

Reading notes by letter names

Read aloud the letter names of notes in the following melodies. This oral reading is to be done in a normal speaking voice with no attempt to produce highness or lowness or duration of the actual sounds of pitches. You are merely to recite names of the pitches and not sing them. Read as quickly as possible. Through additional practice try to increase your speed.

Note to the Instructor: In this exercise, the student should ignore rhythm and any key signature and simply recite the alphabetical names. For example, *America* will be read *ccdbcdeefedcdcbcgggggfeffffedefedcefgafedc*. The objective of this reading practice is to develop the ability for instant recognition of lines and spaces and response by pitch names.

Reminder to the Instructor: In the remaining exercises the student should ignore rhythm and any key signature and simply recite the alphabetical names (without accidentals).

For additional practice, continue the procedure used in Exercise 1.13 by reading letter names of notes in any melodies in Chapter 1 and 3 of *Music for Sight Singing,* third edition, by Robert W. Ottman, Prentice-Hall, Inc., 1986.

(*Return* to page 5)

Pitch:
The Keyboard[1]

The Keyboard

The standard piano keyboard has 88 keys consisting of 52 white keys and 36 black keys. Black keys are found in alternate groups of two and three. This can easily be seen on the keyboard because one group of black keys is always separated from another by a pair of white keys.

Keys at the left of the keyboard sound the lower pitches while keys at the right sound higher pitches. Pitches at the extreme left are said to be at the *bottom* of the keyboard; pitches at the extreme right are said to be at the *top* of

FIGURE 2.1 *Keyboard Groups of Two and Three Black Keys.*

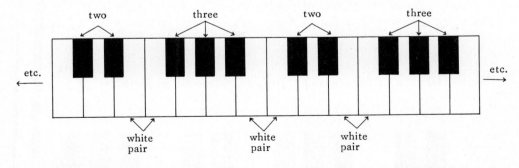

1. Studies in this chapter can be accomplished from the given illustrations and reinforced by application to a real keyboard when available. Only Exercises 2.12-2.15 (optional) require an actual keyboard.

FIGURE 2.2 *The Standard Piano Keyboard.*

bottom—lower pitches

higher pitches-top

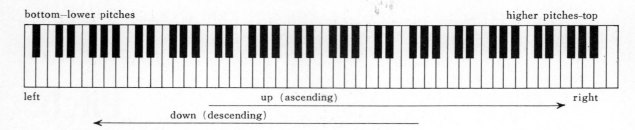

left

up (ascending)

right

down (descending)

the keyboard. Accordingly, when looking from right to left, you look *down* the keyboard; when looking from left to right, you look *up* the keyboard.

Each white and black key of the keyboard is identified by name. First, we shall learn the *names of white keys*.

Names of White Keys

White keys are named with the seven letters of the musical alphabet. The white key at the far left side, at the bottom of the keyboard, is named A. The next white key to the right of A is named with the next letter of the alphabet, B. This application of the alphabet in naming white keys continues in order up the keyboard. After G, which is the seventh and last letter of the musical alphabet, A occurs again. This process is repeated through all succeeding white keys, ending with the highest pitch C at the top of the keyboard.

FIGURE 2.3 *Names of the White Keys on the Piano.*

Observe that any C is located at the immediate left of any group of two black keys. When studying the keyboard in more detail, we will often use the pitch C as a point of orientation, or as a starting point when playing at the keyboard.

The C nearest the middle of the keyboard is called *middle C*. Middle C on the piano corresponds to middle C on the great staff (also see Figs. 1.7 and 1.8 of Chapter 1).

FIGURE 2.4 *Location of C at Left of Two Black Keys.*

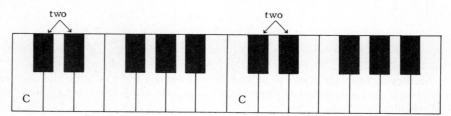

FIGURE 2.5 *Middle C on the Keyboard and Great Staff.*

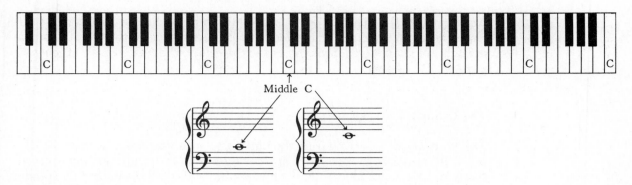

In Figure 2.6 pitches of white keys to the right of (above) middle C are represented as notes in ascending order on lines and spaces of the staff.

In Figure 2.7 pitches of white keys to the left of (below) middle C are represented as notes in descending order on lines and spaces of the staff.

FIGURE 2.6 *White Keys Above Middle C and Notation on the Staff.*

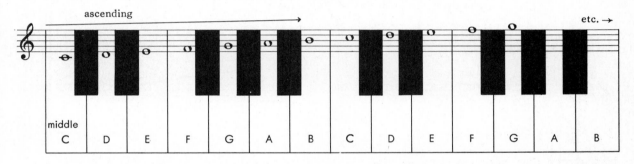

FIGURE 2.7 *White Keys Below Middle C and Notation on the Staff.*

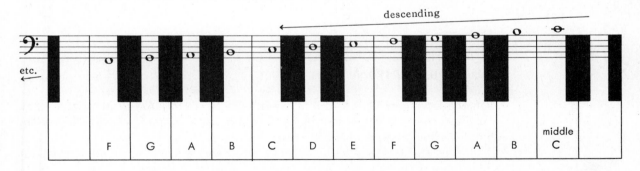

**EXERCISES
2.1, 2.2**

We have now named all the *white keys* of the keyboard with special attention given to the location of C's and, in particular, to the location of middle C. And we have found out how white-key pitches are notated on the staff. *Black keys* are also to be named, but not until we have learned about *intervals* and *accidentals*.

Intervals

An *interval* is the distance between two different pitches, or between two different notes on the staff, or between two different keys on the piano.[2] For the present, we shall study three intervals: the *octave,* the *half step,* and the *whole step.*

The Octave

The word *octave* is derived from the Latin *octo,* meaning *eight.* Look at the keyboard illustration, Figure 2.5. Considering any C as 1 and counting consecutively up the white keys to 8, we find we have arrived at another C. 1 and 8 have the same letter name. This interval of eight degrees, from C to C, is called an octave. In similar fashion it can be shown that the interval from any pitch to the next pitch of the same letter name, either up or down, is an octave.[3] For example, from A up to the next A is an octave, or, from A down to the next A is an octave.

The octave is located on the staff in a similar fashion. Call any note 1 and count up to 8 on consecutive lines and spaces and you will arrive at another note with the same letter name. Calling any note 8 and counting down to 1 also produces the interval of the octave.

FIGURE 2.8 *Octaves.*

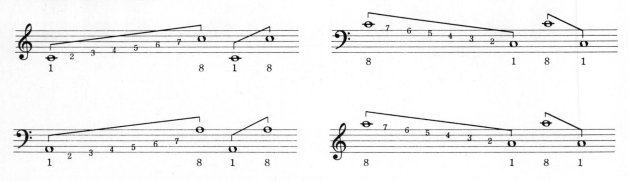

Half Steps and Whole Steps

On the keyboard, a *half step* is the interval from *any key to its adjacent key,* whether that key is white or black. See Figure 2.9. From C, a white key, to the next higher pitch, a black key, is a half step.

From this black key to the adjacent white key above is a half step. From any black key to the adjacent white key is a half step. Notice that there is no black key between E and F or between B and C; therefore, these adjacent white keys are half steps apart.

2. Musical intervals are actually acoustical, but the graphic and spatial aspects of notation and the keyboard are commonly used by musicians in relating to intervallic concepts. Intervals are treated as ratios of frequencies in Appendix 1, *Elementary Acoustics.*
3. Pitches with the same letter name but located at different places on the staff can be differentiated by a system known as *octave registers.* See Appendix 2.

FIGURE 2.9 *Half Steps on the Keyboard.*

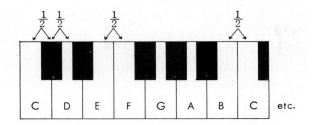

**EXERCISES
2.3, 2.4**

Two half steps in succession equal *one step,* usually called a *whole step.* See Figure 2.10. C to D is a whole step, as the black key in between produces two half steps. Because of the irregularity of the keyboard, with its black keys in groups of two and three, whole steps on the keyboard are found in three different combinations of white and black keys. Whole steps exist (1) from one white key to the next white key, (2) between a white and black key or (3) between a black and another black key.

FIGURE 2.10 *Whole Steps on the Keyboard.*

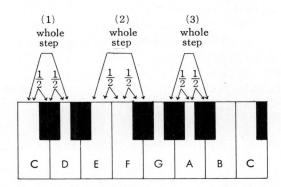

1. A whole step between a white key and another white key.
2. A whole step between a white key and a black key.
3. A whole step between a black key and another black key.

In Chapter 4, half steps and whole steps will be studied further.

Accidentals

An accidental is a symbol (sign) which alters the pitch of a note. There are five different accidentals.

1. The *sharp,* ♯, raises the pitch of a note one half step.
2. The *flat,* ♭, lowers the pitch of a note one half step.
3. The *natural,* ♮, cancels a preceding accidental.
4. The *double sharp,* ×, raises the pitch of a note two half steps or one whole step.
5. The *double flat,* ♭♭, lowers the pitch of a note two half steps or one whole step.

EXERCISE 2.5

FIGURE 2.11 *Accidentals.*

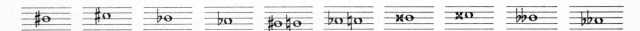

In music writing, the accidental is placed immediately to the left of the note to be altered and precisely on the same line or space of the staff occupied by the note.

When an accidental is to be written in notation, it is, without exception, placed *before* the note as in Figure 2.11. But in speaking the name of an altered note the accidental comes *after* the letter name.

Therefore,   is spoken, "C sharp."

At first, we shall study only sharps and flats. Later, the remaining accidentals will be studied. We are now ready to employ sharps and flats to determine the *names of black keys* of the keyboard.

Names of Black Keys

On the piano keyboard, black keys are named in relationship to the white keys. The black key one half step above C is named *C sharp.* The black key one half step below D is named *D flat.* Observe that the same black key is named both C♯ and D♭. (*Note:* Beginning with Figure 2.12, many illustrations of the keyboard show without color keys which are ordinarily black. This procedure allows information to be placed in the outlined space representing a black key. In Figure 2.12, "C♯" and "D♭" are "black" keys.)

FIGURE 2.12 *Naming the Black Key C♯ and D♭.*

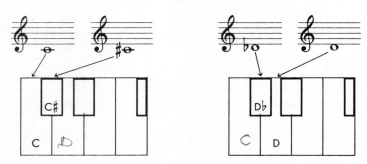

The other black keys are named in a similar manner. For example, the black key one half step above D is D♯; the black (same) key a half step below E is E♭. Figure 2.13 shows names of black and white keys and their representation on the staff.

You have noticed that each black key has two different names. To describe this and similar situations we use the term *enharmonic.*

Enharmonic Spellings

An enharmonic spelling occurs when one and the same pitch has different spellings. For example, C♯ and D♭ are enharmonic spellings (See Figure 2.12); they are played on the piano by the same black key. White keys may also have

FIGURE 2.13a *The Keyboard and Treble Notes on the Staff.*

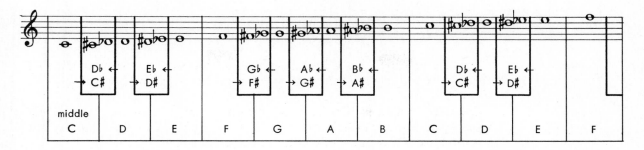

EXERCISE 2.6

FIGURE 2.13b *The Keyboard and Bass Notes on the Staff.*

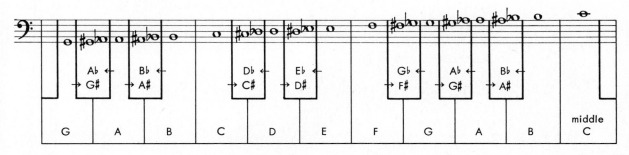

*EXERCISES
2.7, 2.8, 2.9*

enharmonic spellings, either by the use of ♯ or ♭, or ✗ or ♭♭. Any pitch or any key on the keyboard may have an enharmonic spelling as discussed in later chapters.

*EXERCISES
2.10, 2.11*

Playing, Ear Training, and Singing

The first statement in the first chapter of this book, "Obviously the most important aspect of music is its sound," should not be forgotten in the myriad written exercises. At the end of this chapter, exercises dealing with sound, playing at the keyboard, ear training, and singing, are provided. Such exercises in no way impinge on that unique instruction provided by the private teacher of performance. Rather, these exercises involve only the application of theoretical concepts studied in the text.

*EXERCISES
2.12, 2.13,
2.14, 2.15*

EXERCISE 2.1

Names of white keys

Write in names of white keys. C is given.

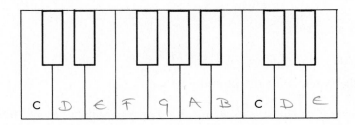

EXERCISE 2.2

Locating C and naming white keys

Write in names of white keys. Locate C first.

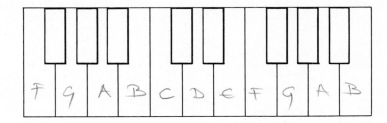

(*Return* to page *17*)

EXERCISE 2.3

Locating half steps above white keys

Indicate with an arrow the key which is one half step above each white key. One example of a half step is illustrated by the arrow which points from a white key to the black key above. Remember that a half step may also occur from one white key to another white key.

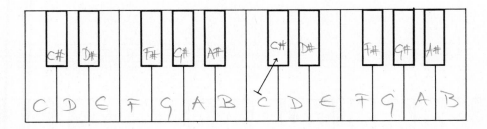

EXERCISE 2.4

Locating half steps below white keys

Indicate with an arrow the key which is one half step below each white key.

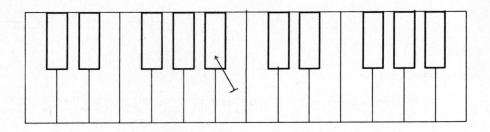

(*Return* to page *19*)

EXERCISE 2.5

Drawing the symbols for sharps and flats

For practice, on the staves below, draw additional sharps and flats, each on the same line or space as the given sharp or flat.

In drawing the symbol for the flat, notice that the length of the vertical line (called *stem*) is approximately equal to the distance of two and one-half spaces of the staff.

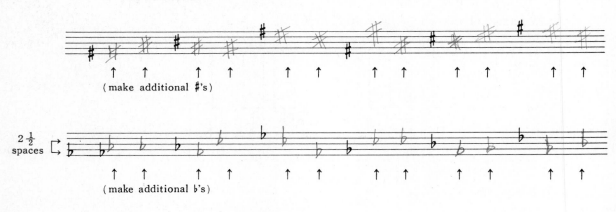

(*Return* to page *20*)

EXERCISE 2.6

Relating half steps on the staff (treble) to the keyboard

Indicate with arrows, as illustrated, the keys which would play the given notes.

a) ascending

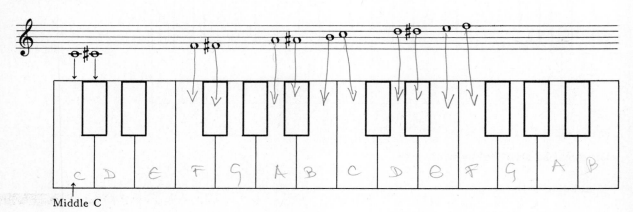

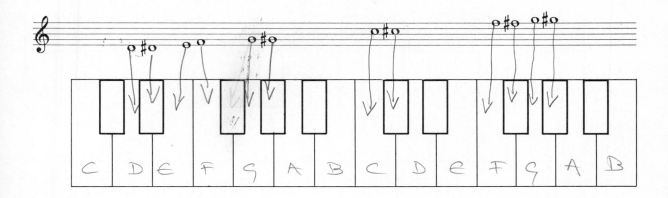

b) descending

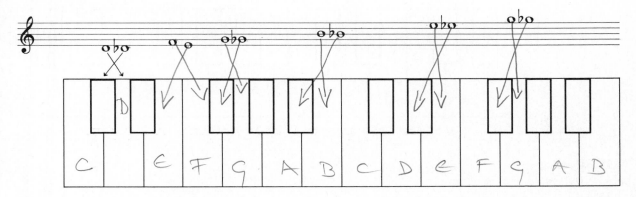

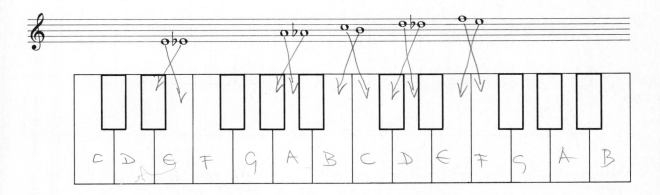

(*Return* to page *21*)

EXERCISE 2.7

Relating half steps on the staff (bass) to the keyboard

Indicate with arrows, as illustrated, the keys which would play the given notes.

25

a) ascending

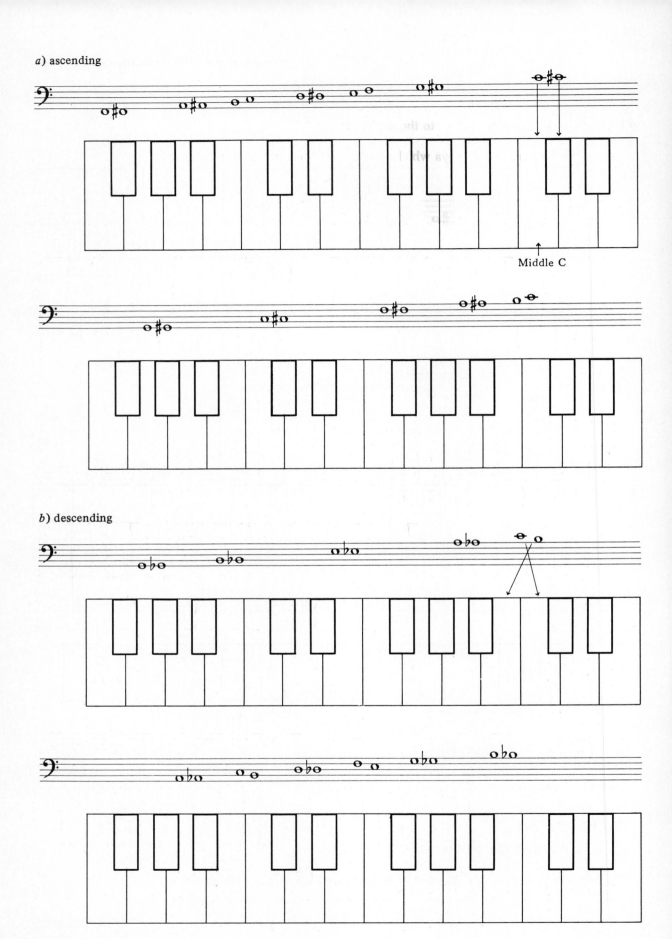

Middle C

b) descending

26

EXERCISE 2.8

Relating notes on the staff (treble) to the keyboard

Indicate with arrows the keys which would play the given notes.

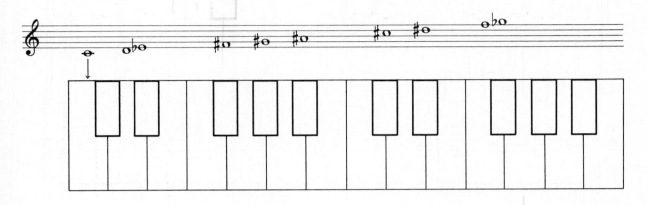

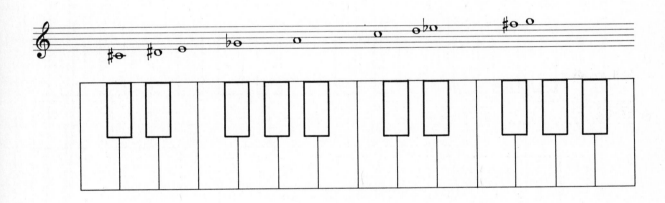

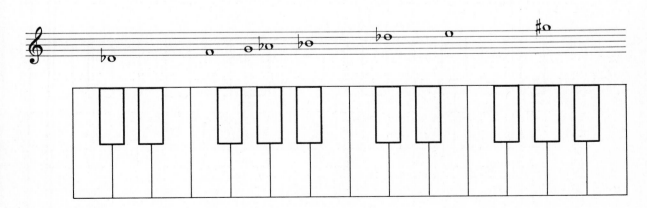

EXERCISE 2.9

Relating notes on the staff (bass) to the keyboard

Indicate with arrows the keys which would play the given notes.

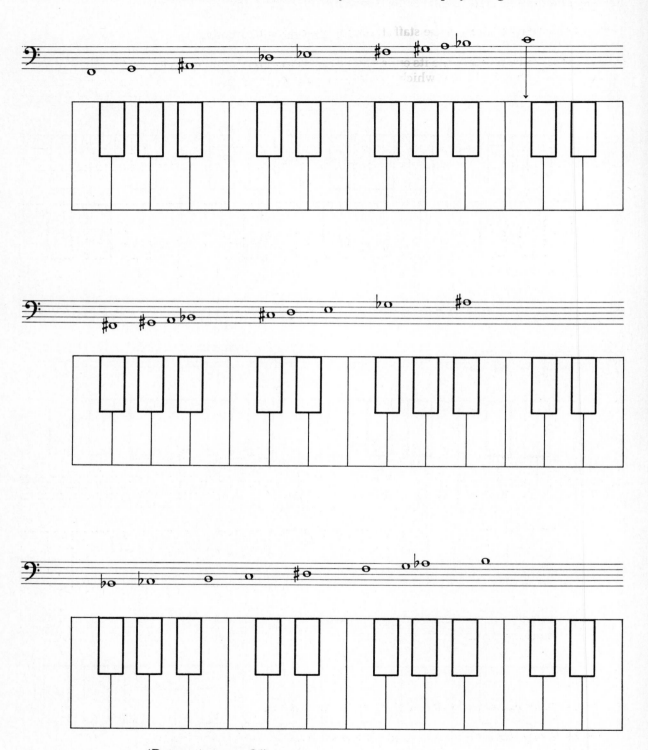

(*Return* to page *21*)

EXERCISE 2.10

Relating enharmonic notes on the staff (treble) to the keyboard

Beside each given note write its enharmonic equivalent. Indicate by arrows, as illustrated, the single key which would play both notes.

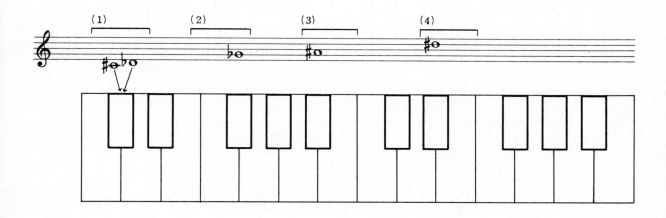

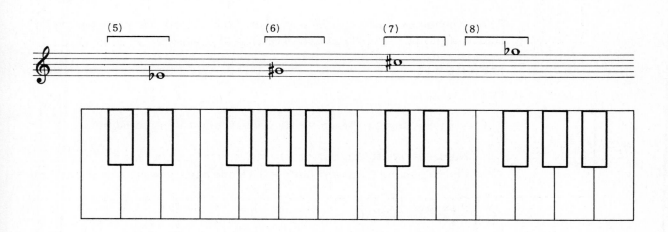

EXERCISE 2.11

Relating enharmonic notes on the staff (bass) to the keyboard

Beside each given note write its enharmonic equivalent. Indicate by arrows, as illustrated, the single key which would play both notes.

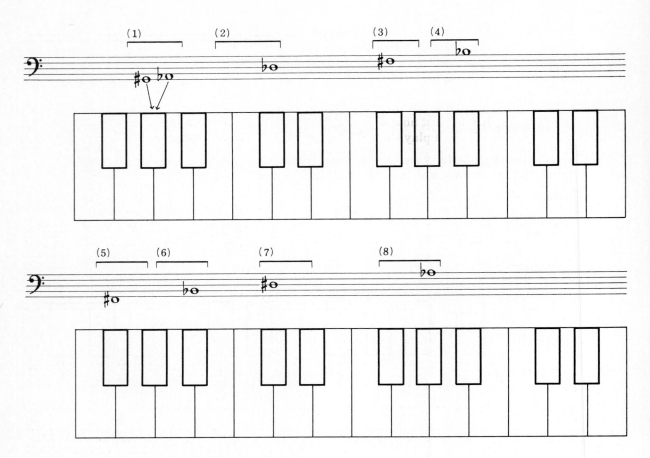

(*Return* to page *21*)

Playing Exercises at the Keyboard

The following exercises will be played at the keyboard. They are planned so that you can practice without the presence of a teacher.

EXERCISE 2.12

Playing white keys

Play on the keyboard each written note. Follow this procedure:

1. Name the written note.
2. Place finger on piano key having the same name and pitch as the written note.
3. Play key.

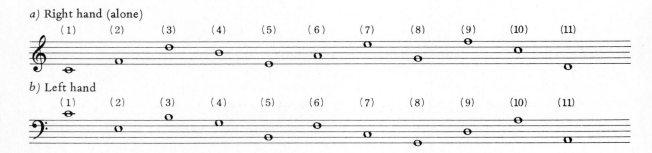

a) Right hand (alone)

b) Left hand

EXERCISE 2.13

Playing half steps

Find the white key for the first note of each pair by following the procedure outlined in Exercise 2.12. Then play the half step above or below according to the notation.

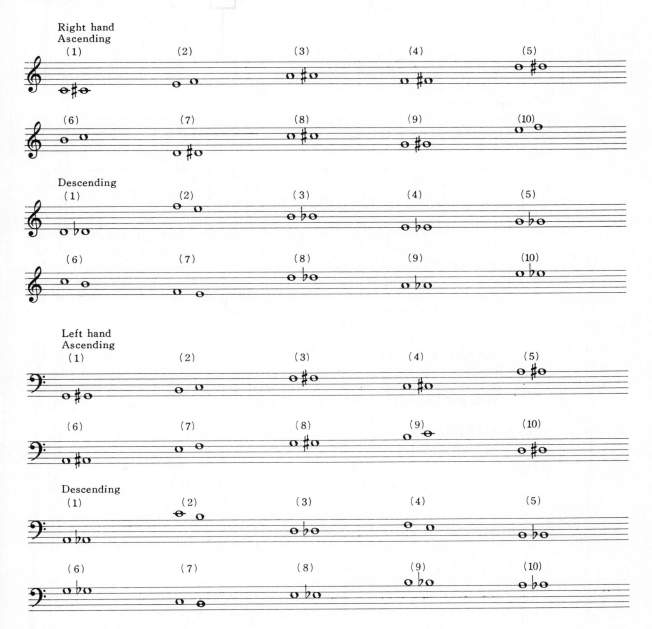

EXERCISE 2.14

Playing any white or black key from written notes on the staff

Play each written note on the keyboard. Each accidental refers only to the note immediately following it.

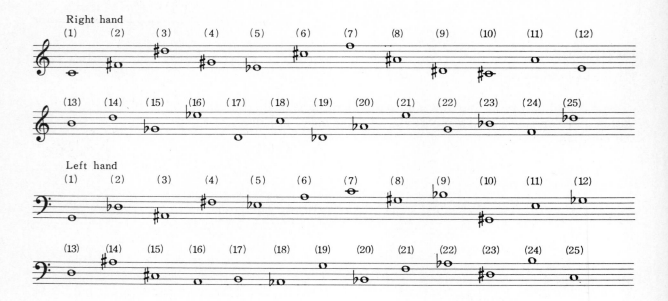

EXERCISE 2.15

Ear training and singing: matching tones

Play each written note individually on the keyboard. After you play a note, sing the same pitch using the neutral syllable *la*. Listen carefully to determine whether the pitch you sing is identical to the one played. This is called *matching the tone*. Women should match the tones of the treble clef pitches; men should match the tones of the bass clef pitches. If at first you find that you are hesitant or unsure in matching tones, continue to practice this exercise in order to acquire the ability for instant and sure response.

Note to the Instructor: Listen carefully to determine that the matched tones are unisons. Matching tones one or more octaves distant will be practiced in the following chapter. If full class participation with both women and men is desired, *a)* and *b)* can be sung at the same time. In this case, play each pitch in both treble and bass before class response.

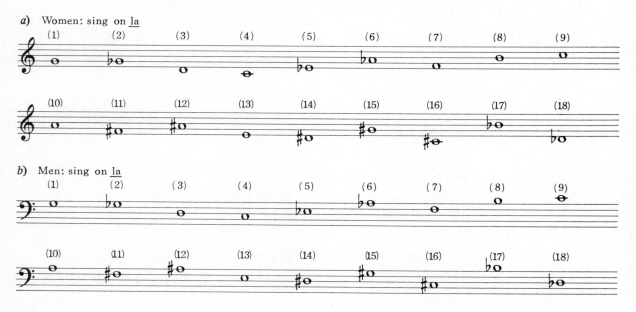

(To continue the study of **Pitch,** *go directly* to **Chapter 4,** page *43*)

CHAPTER THREE

Time

The Construction of Notes
Note Values
The Relationship of Notes to Each Other
Notation of Rests

Following the introduction to *pitch* in Chapters 1 and 2, the next element of sound to be studied is *duration,* or *time*. All durations can be represented by written symbols called notes (first described in the footnote on page 3). The function of a note is to indicate both the duration of a musical sound and, when it is placed on a staff, the pitch of a sound. In Chapters 1 and 2, one type of note (○) was used to indicate pitch, but no attempt was made to describe its use in measuring duration. We shall now consider how notes can indicate duration, beginning our study with *the construction of notes.*

The Construction of Notes

The note is made up of one, two, or three elements: (1) the note head; (2) the stem; (3) the flag.

1. The *note head* is a tilted ellipse, white (open) or black.

    FIGURE 3.1 *Note Heads.*

2. The *stem* is a vertical line connected to a note head. When a single note head is placed on the staff below the third line, the stem points up; when the note head is on or above the third line, the stem points down. Point-

FIGURE 3.2 *Stems.*

ing up, the stem is connected to the right side of the note head; pointing down, the stem appears on the left side of the note head. The length of the stem spans three spaces on the staff.

3. The *flag* is placed at the end of the stem. One to three flags are commonly used; four and five flags are infrequently used. Flags always appear to the right of the stems. Only black notes can have flags.

FIGURE 3.3 *Flags.*

EXERCISE 3.1

Groups of two or more similar notes requiring flags are written two different ways: (1) as separate notes with stems and flags,♪ ♪ ♪, or, in place of flags, (2) with the stems of the notes connected by a heavy line called *beam* or *ligature,* ♫♩ . One beam serves the same function as one flag; two beams serve as two flags,♪ ♪ ♪ or ♬♩ , etc.

If several notes of different pitch are beamed together, use a stem direction which is correct for a majority of the notes in the group.

FIGURE 3.4 *Beamed Notes on the Staff.*

EXERCISE 3.2

Note Values

Notes are named according to mathematical relationships to the number 1 (one whole). The open ellipse is called a *whole note* and assigned the value "1." Other notes are named and evaluated in relationship to the whole note. Figure 3.5 shows the names, symbols, and values of commonly used notes.

The Relationship of Notes to Each Other

The relationship of notes to each other is further illustrated in Figure 3.6. Each mathematical value is divided into the next smaller fraction.

Just as a musical sound has duration, so does silence in music have duration. Symbols representing silence are called *rests*.

FIGURE 3.5 *Note Values.*

Name	Note	Value
Whole note	o	1
Half note	♩ or ♪	$\frac{1}{2}$
Quarter note	♩ or ♪	$\frac{1}{4}$
Eighth note	♪ or ♪	$\frac{1}{8}$
Sixteenth note	♬ or ♬	$\frac{1}{16}$
Thirty-second note	♬ or ♬	$\frac{1}{32}$
Sixty-fourth note etc.	♬ or ♬	$\frac{1}{64}$

Infrequently used in modern notation:

Double whole note |o| or ||o|| or   ⊟   2

EXERCISE 3.3

FIGURE 3.6 *Note Divisions.*

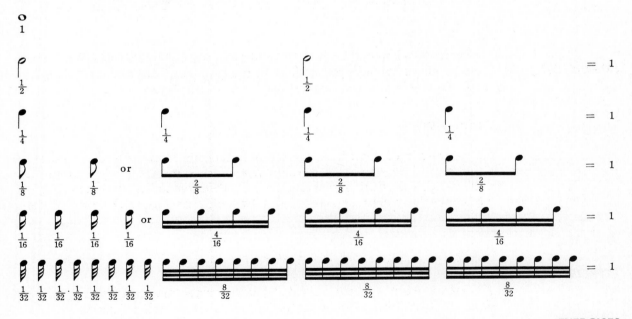

EXERCISES 3.4, 3.5

Notation of Rests

Silence in music is represented by symbols called *rests*. For each note value representing sound, there is a corresponding rest value for silence. Figure 3.7 shows names and symbols for commonly used rests.

FIGURE 3.7 *Rests.*

(margin handwriting: Whole note rest another meaning is whole measure of rest)

Name	Rest	
Whole rest		Whole rest is suspended from the fourth line
Half rest		Half rest sits upon the third line
Quarter rest[1]	⌡ or ⌐	
Eighth rest	⅞	
Sixteenth rest	⅞	
Thirty-second rest	⅞	The stems are slanted The flags point to the left
Sixty-fourth rest	⅞	

Also, corresponding to the double whole note:

Double whole rest

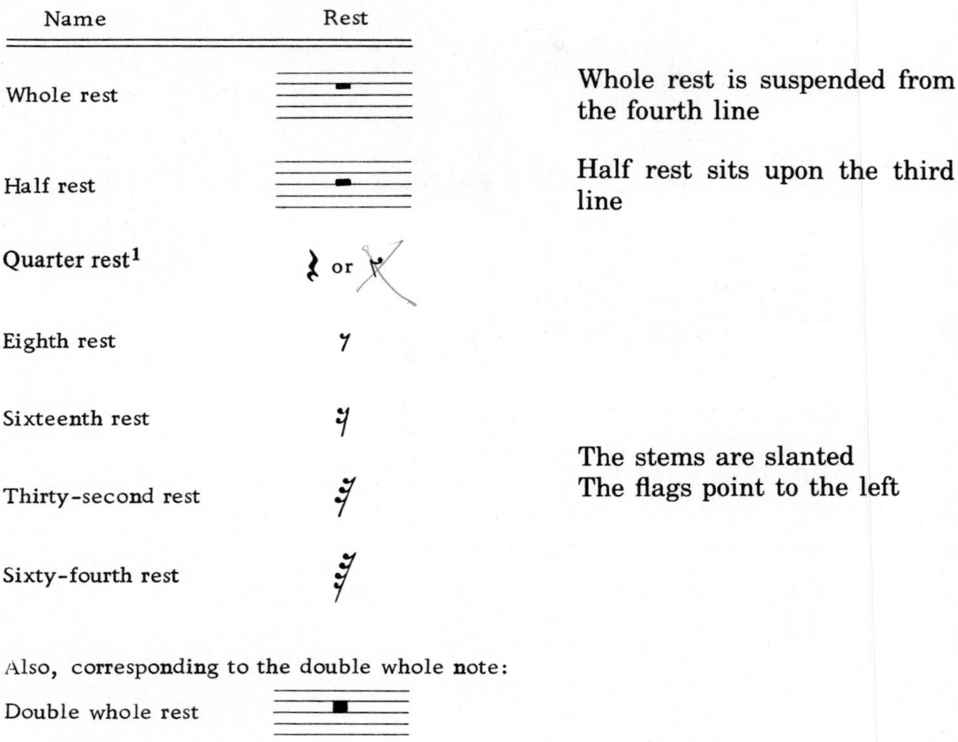

EXERCISES 3.6, 3.7

Figure 3.8 shows different note values and corresponding rests. While notes may be placed on any line or space of the staff, rests are ordinarily found on both the treble and bass staves, as shown in this figure.

FIGURE 3.8 *Notes of Different Values and Corresponding Rests.*

whole	half	quarter	8th	16th	32nd	64th	double whole

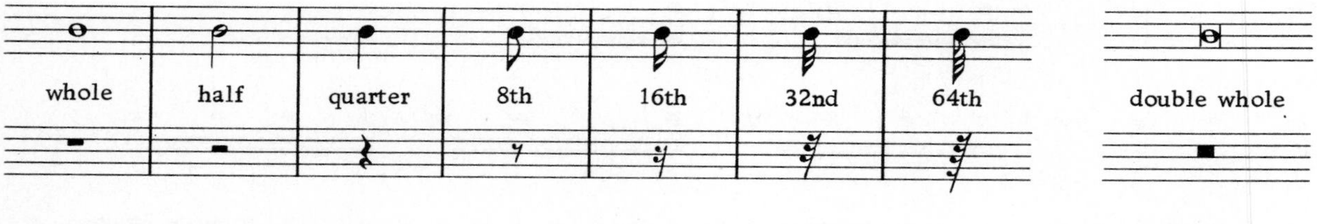

EXERCISE 3.8

1. The quarter rest symbol, ⌐ , may be found particularly in foreign editions of music. Because of possible confusion with the eighth rest, ⅞, its use is not recommended.

Notes and rests presented above are commonly used in music compositions. Many of these are shown in the following short excerpt from Haydn (Figure 3.9).

FIGURE 3.9 *Music Excerpt Showing Many Note Values.*

Haydn, Piano Sonata in E♭ Major, H. XVI:52

* *Tremolo*, played as sixteen 32nd notes, alternating the notes of the octave F.

EXERCISE 3.1

Drawing notes on the staff

After each note, copy the given note above each arrow.

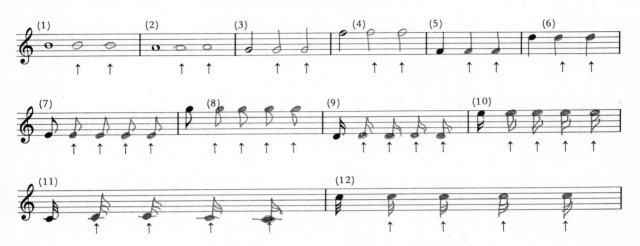

(*Return* to page *34*)

EXERCISE 3.2

Grouping notes with beams

Connect each group of notes with a single beam. Use correct stem direction.

(*Return* to page *34*)

EXERCISE 3.3

Writing various note values

Write the designated note values.

a) on the pitch C

(1) quarter   (2) half   (3) sixteenth   (4) whole   (5) eighth   (6) thirty-second

b) on the pitch B

Example

| (1) half | (2) eighth | (3) whole | (4) thirty-second | (5) quarter | (6) sixteenth |

(*Return* to page *34*)

EXERCISE 3.4

Note divisions

Indicate the division of each given note.

$$\mathbf{o} \;=\; \text{♩} \;\; \text{♩}$$

$$\text{♩} \;=\;$$

$$\text{♩} \;=\;$$

$$\text{♪} \;=\;$$

$$\text{♪} \;=\;$$

$$\text{♪} \;=\;$$

EXERCISE 3.5

Relationship of notes

Fill in the blanks using words only, for example, *two quarter* notes; *eighth* note. Write your answers in the blanks at the right side of the page.

(1) A quarter note equals two
_____8_____ notes.

_____

(2) An _____8_____ note equals two sixteenth notes.

_____

(3) A thirty-second note equals two
_____64_____ notes.

_____

(4) A whole note equals two _____1/2_____
notes.

_____

(5) A _____1/2_____ note equals two quarter notes.

_____

40

NAME _____

(6) A ___1/4___ note equals two eighth
notes.

_____

(7) A sixteenth note equals two
___32___ notes.

_____

(8) A ___1___ note equals two half
notes.

_____

(9) An eighth note equals two
___16___ notes.

_____

(10) A ___16___ note equals two thirty-
second notes.

_____

(*Return* to page *36*)

EXERCISE 3.6

Drawing rests on the staff

After each rest, draw others as indicated. Write the name of the given rest
below the staff.

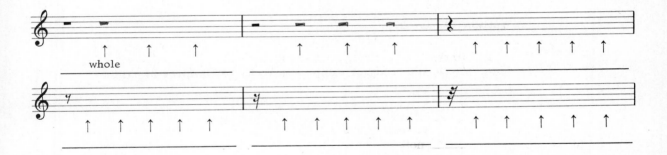

EXERCISE 3.7

Writing various rest values

Write on the staff the rest value designated.

(*Return* to page *36*)

EXERCISE 3.8

Drawing rests corresponding to notes

For each note value, draw and name the corresponding rest.

Note	Corresponding Rest	Name of Rest
		whole rest

(*Return* to page *37*)

(To continue the study of **Time,** *go directly* to **Chapter 5,** page *51*)

CHAPTER FOUR

Pitch:
Major Scales

Design and organization of the sounds of music will become increasingly apparent as you advance in music study. A design, or pattern, commonly used to express organization of pitch is the scale (Latin, *scala*, ladder). A scale is an orderly, graduated arrangement of ascending or descending pitches. There are many kinds of scales used in music, depending on historical period or geographical culture. Most scales in Western music, including those which we will study here, ascend and descend through a series of half steps and whole steps,[1] with each pitch named by a successive letter of the musical alphabet.

For purposes of study, a scale consists of the series of eight notes encompassing the interval of an octave, so that the first and last notes of each scale have identical letter names.[2] Scales differ from each other because the relative placement of the half steps and whole steps within the octave may be different. This can be demonstrated at the piano by choosing a single white key at random and playing a series of eight ascending white keys. If we choose any *A*, the resulting scale would be

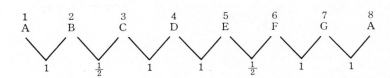

with half steps between 2 and 3 and between 5 and 6, and whole steps between the remaining pitches.[3] If we choose any *C* a different scale would result:

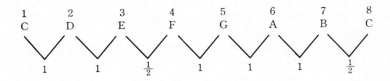

1. Half steps and whole steps were first discussed in Chapter 2, pages 18-19.
2. A scale once established in one octave will sound and be spelled the same at any higher or lower octave.
3. The ascending scale pitches are numbered 1 through 8, and intervals are represented by 1 for a whole step and ½ for a half step.

in which the half steps occur between 3 and 4 and between 7 and 8. By playing white-key scales from each of the seven letter names, seven different scale constructions would result. For present purposes two scale formations, named *major* and *minor,* will be considered. We will begin with the *major scale.*

The Major Scale

The major scale is a series of eight pitches with these intervals between successive pitches: whole step, whole step, half step, whole step, whole step, whole step, and half step (see Figure 4.1).

FIGURE 4.1 *Structure of the Major Scale.*

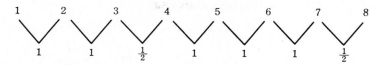

It can be seen that the major scale consists of whole steps except between the third and fourth and the seventh and eighth pitches, where the intervals are half steps.

A scale may be shown on the staff by placing the eight pitches, each known as a scale degree, on eight successive lines and spaces. Each whole step and each half step is represented on the staff by two notes on adjacent lines and spaces. The scale is identified by the relative location of whole steps and half steps, and by the first note of the scale. In Figure 4.2 the scale is major because the half steps occur between 3 and 4 and between 7 and 8 (compare with Fig. 4.1), and it is a C major scale because the first scale degree is C.

FIGURE 4.2 *The C Major Scale.*

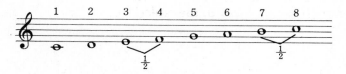

Notice that the major scale starting on C involves only white keys because the half steps 3–4 and 7–8 coincide with the white keys E–F and B–C. The major scale based on C is the only major scale consisting entirely of white keys. The characteristic sound of the major scale can be reproduced by beginning on any pitch name or on any key of the piano. When starting on a pitch other than C, however, we must employ one or more accidentals to maintain the characteristic half step and whole step pattern of the major scale shown first in Figure 4.1. Accidentals are added so that the half steps will appear in their proper location between 3 and 4 and between 7 and 8, and so that the remaining steps will be whole steps. To illustrate, a white key scale on G produces a scale with half steps between 3 and 4 and between 6 and 7:

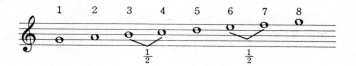

Raising F to F♯ eliminates the half step between 6 and 7 and creates a half step between 7 and 8 so that, with the half step remaining between 3 and 4, the scale is major.

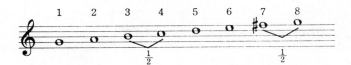

Care should be taken so that incorrect spellings of pitches by enharmonics are not used. In the G major scale shown below, writing G♭ instead of F♯ for the seventh scale degree is incorrect for two reasons: (1) the complete musical alphabet is not employed (the letter F is missing), and (2) the whole step between 6 and 7 does not occur on adjacent staff degrees.

f♯ is erroneously
omitted in the spelling

A white key scale on F produces a scale with half steps between 4 and 5 and between 7 and 8:

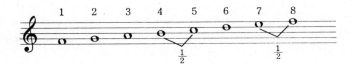

Lowering the B to B♭ produces a half step between 3 and 4 and, with the half step remaining between 7 and 8, the scale is major.

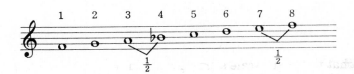

Major scales may begin on black keys, or on letter names containing an accidental. The scale is produced as before, with half steps between 3 and 4 and between 7 and 8, for example,

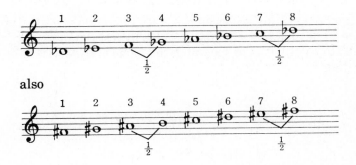

also

Although theoretically a major scale can start on any letter name containing an accidental, for practical purposes, scales that would require more than seven sharps or seven flats are not used. We will not consider scales requiring double sharps or double flats. For example, a major scale on G♯ would require eight sharps: G♯, A♯, B♯, C♯, D♯, E♯, F×, G♯, where F is sharpened twice and indicated as F×.

Since there are but seven letter names, the maximum number of scales containing sharps will be seven, and the maximum number of scales containing flats will also be seven. These, with C major, comprise the fifteen major scales.

FIGURE 4.3 *Table of Major Scales and Numbers of Accidentals.*

Scale	C	G	D	A	E	B	F♯	C♯
Accidentals	none	1♯	2♯	3♯	4♯	5♯	6♯	7♯
Scale		F	B♭	E♭	A♭	D♭	G♭	C♭
Accidentals		1♭	2♭	3♭	4♭	5♭	6♭	7♭

You will observe in Figure 4.3 that there is a definite relationship between the number of accidentals used in a scale and the name of the starting pitch of the scale. If you count *up* five notes from the starting note (and include the starting note), a new scale beginning at this point will have one sharp more than the preceding scale. This additional sharp will always occur on the seventh degree of the new scale.

If you count *down* five notes, the new scale beginning at this point will have one flat more than the preceding scale. This additional flat will always occur on the fourth degree of the new scale.

EXERCISE 4.1

In addition to notating scales on the staff, it is often useful in musical communication to be able to spell (write) scales by letter names with appropriate accidentals. In spelling, as in speaking, the name of the accidental comes after the letter name.

FIGURE 4.4 *Spelling the B♭ Major Scale.*

EXERCISE 4.2   B♭ C D E♭ F G A B♭

CHAPTER FIVE

Time
(continued)

Beats
Tempo
Grouping of Beats
Bar Lines
Measure

In Chapter 3 we studied notation of durations and the mathematical relationships of notes and rests. Next, we will learn how durations of time are measured through beats (pulsations), and how to put these measurements on paper so they can be read by a performer.

Other than mechanical and electronic chronometers, several time-measuring devices or sensations are common to the human experience. The heart normally beats with a regular pulsation, marking off regular units of time. When you walk, each step usually takes the same amount of time as the preceding and following steps, at least until you consciously change your rate of speed. These two physical sensations, among many others, mark off units of time of equal length. For purposes of measuring equal lengths of time in music, these regularly recurring pulsations are called *beats*.

Beats

Beats are regularly recurring physical pulsations which divide time into units of equal length. In your ordinary experiences in music, you have already felt this sensation and expressed yourself by regular tapping of your fingers or your feet, or you have danced or marched in conformity with the beats of the music. We will begin our study of time by experiencing again the sensation of beats. The instructor will play several melodies. Your reaction is simply to tap naturally with the right hand. The melodies you will hear are shown in Figure 5.1. The vertical lines below the staff represent the taps or beats.

FIGURE 5.1 *Tapping Beats.*

(a) M.M. ♩ = 96   Handel, *Joy to the World*

(b) M.M. ♩. = 80   *Oh Dear, What Can the Matter Be?*

(c) M.M. ♩ = 88   *Santa Lucia*

(d) M.M. ♩ = 96   Spilman, *Flow Gently Sweet Afton*

(e) M.M. ♩ = 120   *Jingle Bells*

(f) M.M. ♩ = 100   *Auld Lang Syne*

You may have noticed that you tapped at a different rate of speed for different melodies. This phenomenon is explained by the term *tempo*.

Tempo

Tempo (pl. tempos, or tempi) is the rate of speed of the beats. The faster the succession of beats, the faster is the tempo; the slower the succession of beats, the slower is the tempo. In a fast tempo the beats measure relatively short durations of time; in a slow tempo the beats measure relatively long durations of time. The varying durations of the beat depend on the kind of music and the intent of the composer.

The length of the beat can be precisely measured by a mechanical device known as a metronome, which produces a regular recurring ticking sound. The metronome can be regulated to produce the ticking sound from very fast successions to very slow successions. It is calibrated so that when set on "60" it produces one tick per second; at "120," two ticks per second, etc. Composers often indicate tempo by placing the abbreviation M.M.[1] plus the desired number at the beginning of a piece (for example, M.M. 60).

While listening to music, certain beats are felt more strongly than others. There are heavy beats and light beats; the combinations of heavy and light beats in succession produce *grouping of beats*.

Grouping of Beats

Beats tend to group themselves into regular recurring patterns. Three patterns are commonly found in music: (1) a heavy beat followed by a light beat (duple); (2) a heavy beat followed by two light beats (triple); and (3) a heavy beat followed by three lighter beats with the third beat slightly stronger than the second and fourth (quadruple). See Figure 5.2. As the instructor plays, you will experience these groupings as shown in Figure 5.3. As in Figure 5.2, the vertical lines below the staff represent beats. A long line represents a heavy

---

1. M.M. stands for Mälzel's metronome. Johann N. Mälzel invented the instrument in 1816. It was first used to indicate tempi by Beethoven.

FIGURE 5.2 *Beat Patterns.*

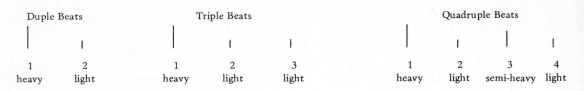

FIGURE 5.3 *Grouping of Beats.*

(a) M.M. ♩ = 96 Duple

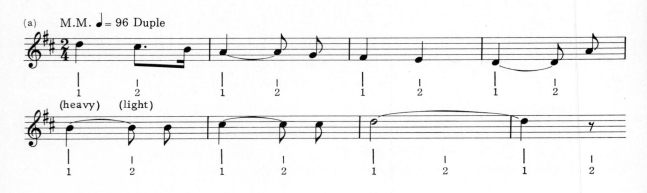

(b) M.M. ♩ = 88 Triple

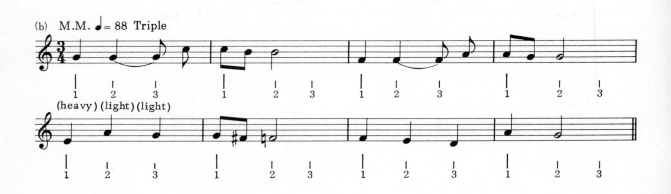

c) M.M. ♩ = 92 Quadruple

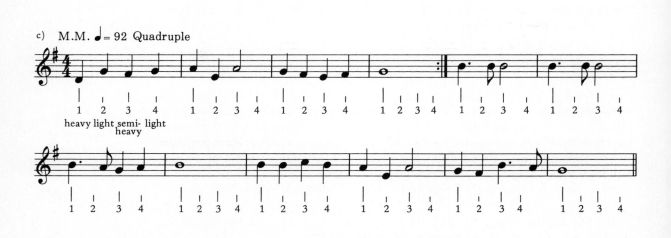

beat, a short line a light beat. When listening to each melody, tap the beats as before with the right hand, but make a stronger tap at the place of each long vertical line and a weaker tap at each short vertical line in accordance with the sensation of heavy and light beats in the music.

It is sometimes difficult in listening to distinguish between groupings of two and groupings of four because the semi-heavy beat on "3" in quadruple can easily be mistaken for the heavy beat "1" in a group of two beats. For a comparison see Figure 5.4.

FIGURE 5.4 *Comparison of Duple and Quadruple Groups of Beats.*

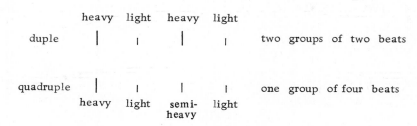

EXERCISES
5.1T, 5.2T

In addition to identifying the grouping of beats by *hearing* relative pulsations in the music, you can *see* (in the music examples throughout this chapter) a simple device which also indicates grouping of beats. This visual aid is the *bar line,* with resulting *measure.*

Bar Lines

A single *bar line* serves to separate one group of beats from the next. It is a vertical line extending across the staff from the bottom to the top lines. A *double bar line* is used at the end of a composition or at the end of a section of a composition.

FIGURE 5.5 *Bar Lines.*

Measure

A measure as seen on the staff is the distance between bar lines. Each measure is heard as a group of beats. "Measure" is included in further study of Time in Chapter 9.

In the following exercise numbers, and throughout this book, the letter T indicates need for a teacher, or tutor, to conduct the drills.

EXERCISE 5.1T

Tapping beats and groupings

Listen to a melody played by the instructor. On the second hearing, tap the beats, making a heavy tap where you hear the heavy beat in the music. Determine whether the beats are in groups of two, three, or four and be prepared to identify the grouping for the piece as "duple," "triple," or "quadruple." For this exercise, use music found in Exercise 5.2T.

EXERCISE 5.2T

Aural identification of groupings of beats

Listen to a melody played by the instructor. On the second hearing, try to recognize the beats without tapping. Identify the grouping of beats as before.

(4)   M. M. 112   Mendelssohn, *Hark the Herald Angels Sing*

(5)   M.M. 104   de Giardini, *Come Thou Almighty King*

(6)   M. M. 104   Lambert, *When Johnny Comes Marching Home*

For additional drill, continue Exercises 5.1T and 5.2T using the following melodies from *Music for Sight Singing* (third edition). Observe the recommended metronome indications.

(1)	87	M.M. ♩ = 108	(7)	246	M.M. ♩ = 116
(2)	97	M.M. ♩ = 116	(8)	267	M.M. ♩. = 63
(3)	176	M.M. ♩. = 76	(9)	511	M.M. ♩. = 80
(4)	223	M.M. ♩ = 100	(10)	522	M.M. ♩ = 120
(5)	238	M.M. ♩ = 138	(11)	530	M.M. ♩ = 142
(6)	239	M.M. ♩ = 108	(12)	537	M.M. ♩ = 104

(*Return* to page *55*)

(To continue the study of **Time,** *go directly* to **Chapter 7,** page 67)

CHAPTER SIX

Pitch: Major Scales (continued)

Names of Scale Degrees

The scale has been shown (in Chapter 4) to be composed of eight successive pitches, each known as a scale degree. The terms *scale tone* and *scale step* are often used synonymously with *scale degree*. For example, in the scale of *C* major, the fifth degree, *G*, may be called the fifth scale tone or fifth scale step. In addition to these general designations, each tone, step or degree of the scale can be identified by a specific name of its own. Here, with a discussion of the significance of each, are the *names of the scale degrees*.

Names of the Scale Degrees

The name of the first scale degree is *tonic* (Greek, *tonikos*[1]). It is the main tone, the tone which gives the scale its identity. In the *C* major scale, *C* is the tonic tone.

Since the tonic is the most important tone, all other degrees are signified by their relationships to it.

Second only to the tonic in importance is the fifth scale tone, which is called *dominant*. It dominates or is dominant to all the scale tones except tonic. The dominant is the fifth degree above tonic. In the C major scale, G is the dominant tone.

1. *tonikos,* stretching, referring to the fact that a string must be stretched to produce a tone. Greek, *tonos,* Latin, *tonus,* tone.

The scale tone five steps below the tonic and ranking next in importance to the dominant is called *subdominant*. The prefix *sub* indicates a tone under or below the tonic.

Notice that while the dominant is five steps above the tonic, the subdominant is five steps below the tonic. In the C major scale, F is the subdominant tone, the fourth scale degree.

The third scale tone, which is midway between the tonic and dominant, is called *mediant*. In the C major scale, E is the mediant tone.

The sixth scale tone, which is the middle or median tone between the tonic and subdominant, is called *submediant*. Notice that while the mediant is three steps above the tonic, the submediant is three steps below the tonic. In the C major scale, A is the submediant tone.

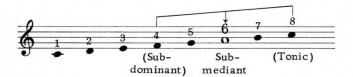

The seventh tone in the major scale, because of its strong tendency to lead upward to the tonic, is called *leading tone*.[2] In the C major scale, B is the leading tone.

The second scale tone, the scale degree immediately above tonic, is called *supertonic*. Notice that while the leading tone is the tone just below tonic, the supertonic is the tone just above tonic. In the C major scale, D is the supertonic tone.

2. Sometimes called *subtonic* since it is the tone immediately below the tonic.

60

In ascending order, the names of the scale tones are shown in Figure 6.1.

FIGURE 6.1 *Names of the Scale Tones.*

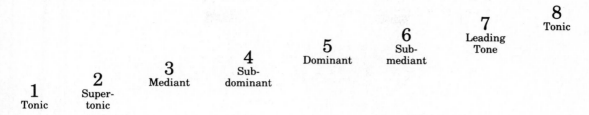

In Figure 6.2, names of the scale tones in ascending and consecutive order are shown for C major.

FIGURE 6.2 *Names of the Scale Tones, C Major.*

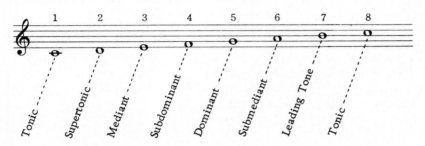

Scale tone names are applied in similar manner for all major scales.

EXERCISE 6.1

Naming scale tones (degrees)

a) Supply the names of the scale tones (degrees). For D major:

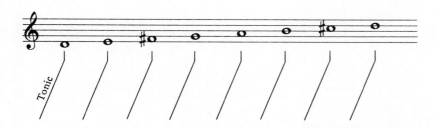

b) Write the B♭ major scale on the staff, ascending for one octave, and name the scale degrees:

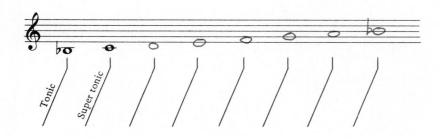

EXERCISE 6.2

Naming scale degrees

Following number 1 (tonic), scale degree numbers are given in random order. Write the name for each:

Scale Degree	Name
1	tonic
5	_____
4	_____
3	_____
6	_____
7	_____
2	_____

EXERCISE 6.3

Identifying scale degrees

Write the name of the scale degree below each note on the staff. The first note on each staff is the tonic note of the scale.

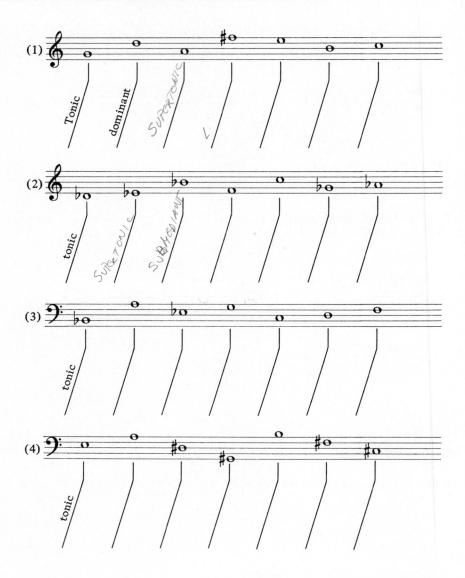

EXERCISE 6.4

Identifying scale degrees

Give the pitch name for each scale degree listed when the tonic is identified.

(1) Tonic _____ F _____
    Mediant _____ A _____
    Submediant _____ D _____
    Leading Tone _____ E _____
    Supertonic _____ G _____
    Dominant _____ C _____
    Subdominant _____ B _____

(2) Tonic _____ B _____
    Submediant _____
    Supertonic _____ C _____
    Leading Tone _____
    Subdominant _____
    Mediant _____ D _____
    Dominant _____

(3) Tonic _____ E♭ _____
    Leading tone _____ D _____
    Dominant _____ B♭ _____
    Supertonic _____ F _____
    Submediant _____ C _____
    Subdominant _____ A♭ _____
    Mediant _____ G _____

(4) Tonic _____ G♭ _____
    Subdominant _____ C♭ _____
    Mediant _____ B♭ _____
    Submediant _____ E♭ _____
    Supertonic _____ A♭ _____
    Dominant _____ D♭ _____
    Leading Tone _____ F _____

To continue the study of **Pitch,** *go directly* to **Chapter 8,** page 75)

CHAPTER SEVEN

Time (continued)

Divisions of Beats
Simple Beat
Compound Beat
Meter

In Chapter 5, you were asked to listen to a number of musical examples. One characteristic common to all the melodies was the sensation of a regular recurring beat. Readily noticeable, however, was the fact that in different melodies the beats grouped themselves in different combinations of two, three, or four. Now we will consider another characteristic quality of the beat, the sensation of *divisions of beats*.

Divisions of Beats

There are two varieties of the beat, each identified by the way the beat duration can be divided. You can demonstrate this when listening to a melody by making either two or three taps with the left hand to each tap in the right hand. Whether you tap two or three in the left hand will be sensed from the sound of the melody itself, as will be shown in the following discussion of *simple* and *compound beats*.

Simple Beat

A beat which can be divided into two parts is called a *simple beat*. Listen to the melody in Figure 7.1. On the second hearing tap the beats in the right hand as done previously and as shown in Step 1. On the third hearing tap twice with the left hand for each tap in the right hand as shown in Step 2.

In Figure 7.1 the taps in the right hand determine the duration of each beat. The taps in the left hand divide each of these durations into two equal parts. This division is called *simple division of the beat*.

FIGURE 7.1 *Tapping Simple Division.*

Compound Beat

A beat that can be divided into three parts is called a *compound beat*. Listen to the melody in Figure 7.2. On the second hearing tap the beats in the right hand as done previously and as shown in Step 1. On the third hearing tap three times with the left hand for each tap in the right hand as shown in Step 2. The left hand is *dividing the beat* into three parts; this division is called the *compound division of the beat*.

FIGURE 7.2 *Tapping Compound Division.*

In an earlier chapter we recognized groupings of beats in patterns of two, three, or four; in this chapter we have examined the two varieties of beats. We have now found three different groupings of beats and two different divisions for each beat, making a total of six possible combinations for groupings of beats and their divisions. The terminology for identifying these various combinations comes under the general term *meter*.

Meter

In music, *meter* is the systematic grouping of beats and their divisions in regularly recurring patterns of pulsations. Meter is described as being *duple, triple,* or *quadruple* according to the grouping of beats, and *simple* or *compound* according to the division of each beat. Therefore, the six possible meter designations are:

FIGURE 7.3 *Meter Designations.*[1]

1. duple simple   4. duple compound
2. triple simple   5. triple compound
3. quadruple simple   6. quadruple compound

The sensations for these six meter designations can be manifested by tapping: the right hand taps the particular grouping of beats, as practiced in Chapter 5, while the left hand taps the particular division of each beat. Figure 7.4 shows diagrams for tapping the various combinations.

FIGURE 7.4 *Diagrams for Tapping Meter.*

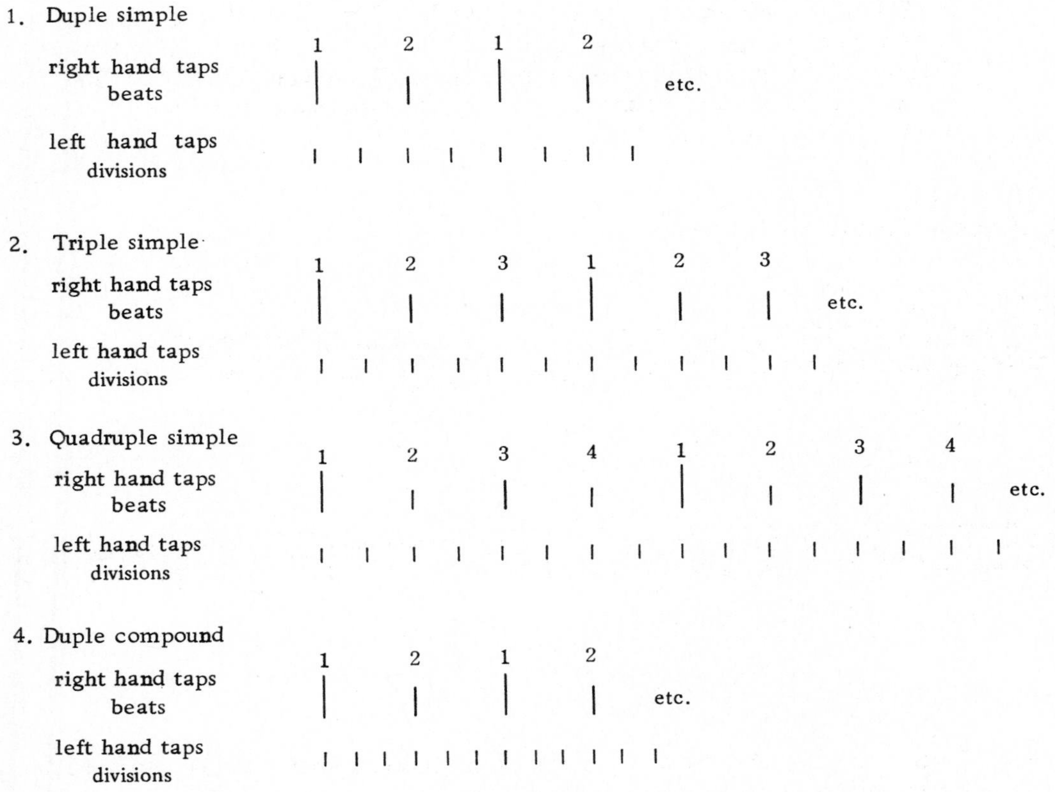

1. Some theorists prefer to reverse these designations, e.g., simple duple, compound triple, etc.

5. Triple compound

right hand taps
beats

left hand taps
divisions

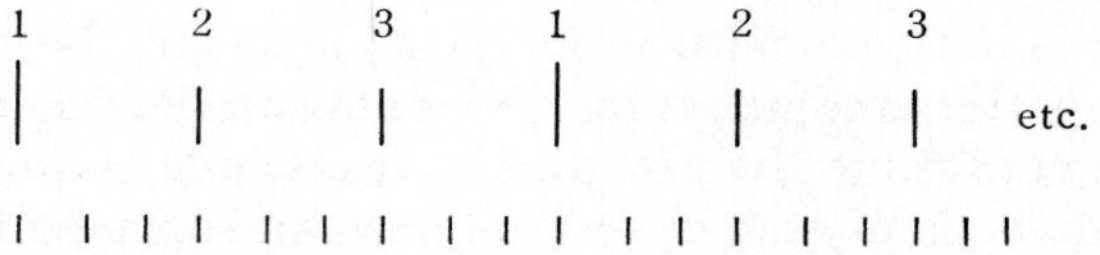

6. Quadruple compound

right hand taps
beats

left hand taps
divisions

How these meters are expressed as time signatures is included in Chapter 9.

EXERCISE 7.1T

Tapping simple meters without music

The instructor will announce a meter designation as duple simple, or triple simple, or quadruple simple. The student taps the beats and background as shown in Figure 7.4. Using the metronome, the tempo for the beats should neither be slower than M.M. 52 nor faster than M.M. 116.

EXERCISE 7.2T

Tapping simple meters with music

Listen to a melody played by the instructor. On the second hearing tap the groupings of beats with the right hand. On the third playing add the background of two with the left hand. Be prepared to identify the meter by one of the three simple meter designations.

(1) M.M. ♩ = 84

France

(2) M.M. ♩ = 76

de Curtis, *Come Back to Sorrento*

(3) M.M. ♩ = 100

Ukraine

(4) M.M. ♩ = 76

Franck, Symphony in D Minor

71

(5) M.M. ♩ = 100   France

(6) M.M. ♩ = 108   Brahms, Hungarian Dance No. 5

EXERCISE 7.3T

Tapping compound meters without music

The instructor will announce a meter designation as duple compound, or triple compound, or quadruple compound. The student taps the beats and division as shown in Figure 7.4. Using the metronome, the tempo for the beats should be neither slower than M.M. 46 nor faster than M.M. 96.

EXERCISE 7.4T

Tapping compound meters with music

Listen to a melody played by the instructor. On the second hearing tap the groupings of beats with the right hand. On the third playing add the division of three with the left hand. Be prepared to identify as either duple compound or triple compound. (Quadruple compound time is not frequently used in music composition since one quadruple unit usually sounds like two duple units. For this reason, no quadruple compound meter is included in this exercise.)

(1) M.M. ♩. = 54   Barnby, *Sweet and Low*

(2) M.M. ♩. = 66   Mendelssohn, *Greeting at Morn*

(3) M.M. ♩. = 52   *Drink to Me Only with Thine Eyes*

(4) M.M. ♩.= 64

(5) M.M. ♩.= 66

EXERCISE 7.5T

Tapping simple or compound meters with music

Listen to a melody played by the instructor. It may be in either a simple or compound meter as selected by the instructor. On the second hearing tap both the groupings of beats and the divisions, and identify as before. (There will be no quadruple compound meter included in this exercise.)

(1) M.M. ♩.= 48

Offenbach, *Barcarolle*

(2) M.M. ♩= 100

England

(3) M.M. ♩.= 60

Foster, *Beautiful Dreamer*

(4) M.M. ♩ = 50   MacDowell, *To a Wild Rose*

(5) M.M. ♩ = 76   Rimsky-Korsakov, *Song of India*

For additional drill, continue Exercise 7.5T using the following melodies from *Music for Sight Singing*.

(1)	73	M.M. ♩ = 92	(9)	346	M.M. ♪ = 100
(2)	84	M.M. ♩ = 108	(10)	364	M.M. ♩ = 86
(3)	96	M.M. ♩ = 116	(11)	372	M.M. ♩ = 60
(4)	192	M.M. ♩. = 92	(12)	374	M.M. ♩. = 69
(5)	194	M.M. ♩. = 84	(13)	456	M.M. ♩. = 80
(6)	225	M.M. ♩ = 100	(14)	483	M.M. ♩. = 69
(7)	230	M.M. ♩ = 112	(15)	522	M.M. ♩ = 112
(8)	248	M.M. ♩ = 92	(16)	526	M.M. ♩ = 80

(To continue the study of **Time,** *go directly* to **Chapter 9,** page *85*)

CHAPTER EIGHT

Pitch: Major Scales (continued)

Playing Major Scales at the Keyboard
Singing Major Scales

With our knowledge of the keyboard (studied in Chapter 2) and major scales (studied in Chapters 4 and 6), we will now set out to perform scales on the piano and to sing them. In performing a scale it is of utmost importance to keep in mind the series of whole steps and half steps that produce the major scale. Though this may not seem of particular importance when playing the scale on the piano, where the keys play fixed pitches, it becomes essential in singing or when playing such instruments as violin or trombone where the performer is responsible for fixing the pitches, or in recognizing by ear whether a series of pitches produces a major scale or some other variety of scale. Development of the ability to produce or to differentiate whole steps and half steps is an important result of *playing scales at the keyboard*.

Playing Scales at the Keyboard[1]

The C Major Scale. By playing the white key C and the next seven white keys above it, a C major scale is produced. Playing only white keys from this given pitch C automatically places the half steps in their correct scale locations, between 3 and 4 and between 7 and 8, as shown in Figure 8.1.

---

1. Keyboard performance of scales may be studied from one of two points of view: (1) simply for knowledge of scale construction and sound, in which case the fingering of the scale is not a primary consideration; or (2) for achieving skill in performance, in which case fingering is a vital consideration. Correct scale fingerings are shown in Appendix 4, pages 287-88.

FIGURE 8.1 *Playing the C Major Scale.*

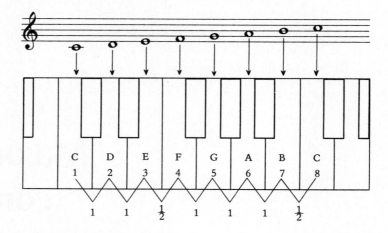

To Play Major Scales Other than C

1. Use the same pattern of whole steps and half steps as in the C major scale.

2. Use a black key when the note name includes an accidental (except in the scales of F♯, C♯, G♭, and C♭, which are described below).

3. Begin the scale on a black key when the tonic note includes an accidental (except in the scale of C♭ major). See the E♭ scale in Figure 8.2.

4. Expect various combinations of black and white keys to produce whole steps. In Figure 8.2:

E♭ to F	is black to white
F to G	is white to white
A♭ to B♭	is black to black

FIGURE 8.2 *Playing the E♭ Major Scale.*

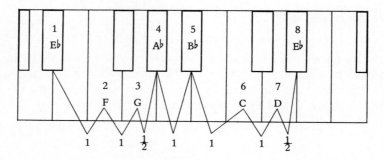

In the remaining scales of F♯, C♯, G♭, and C♭, some note names using accidentals must be played on white keys. In previous study you learned that black keys can be spelled enharmonically. All white keys may also carry enharmonic spellings, but at this time we shall limit ourselves to those half steps using the white keys E-F and B-C. Enharmonic equivalents of these are necessary for the last four scales.

FIGURE 8.3 *E♯, B♯, F♭ and C♭ on the Keyboard.*

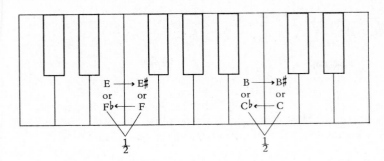

The scales of F♯, C♯, G♭, and C♭ will make use of the following enharmonic spellings. For example, the F♯ major scale uses the enharmonic white key E♯ (see Figure 8.4). The C♯ scale will use E♯ and B♯, the G♭ scale will use C♭, and the C♭ scale, starting on the enharmonic white key C♭, will use F♭.

FIGURE 8.4 *Playing the F♯ Major Scale.*

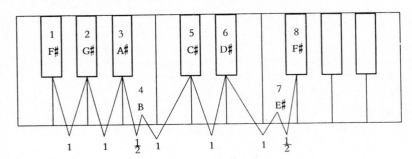

EXERCISES 8.1, 8.2, 8.3

Singing Major Scales

Singing is ordinarily the vocal performance of a musical setting of a literary text, usually poetry, called a song. However, in a course of study in music theory and in the preparation and training of a musician, the student will often be required to sing, not songs with words having artistic expression, but exercises with vocal sounds having theoretical significance. Singing major scales is such an exercise. The vocal sounds can be expressed three ways:

(1) *By numbers.* Figure 8.5 shows application for the C major scale.

FIGURE 8.5 *Singing the Scale by Numbers, C Major.*

(2) *By letter names.* Figure 8.6 shows application for the D major scale. When a letter name includes an accidental, sing on two repeated pitches, e.g., "f-sharp."

77

FIGURE 8.6 *Singing the Scale by Letter Names, D Major.*

Sing: d   e   f♯   g   a   b   c♯   d   d   c♯   b   a   g   f♯   e   d

(3) *By syllables.* Singing with syllables is known as *solmization.* Two important systems of solmization are known as *tonic sol-fa* and *solfeggio.*[2] Figure 8.7 shows a solmization of the C major scale.

FIGURE 8.7 *Singing the Scale by Syllables, C Major.*

Sing: do   re   mi   fa   sol   la   ti   do   do   ti   la   sol   fa   mi   re   do

The syllables are pronounced:

do—*doe*
re—*ray*
mi—*me*
fa—*fah*
sol—*soh*
la—*lah*
ti—*tee*

EXERCISE 8.4

2. In the tonic sol-fa system the syllables are moveable, that is, "do" is always the tonic note of the scale. In solfeggio, the syllables are fixed: C, for example, is always "do" regardless of its location in the scale. This text will make use only of tonic sol-fa.

Accounts of the invention of a system of solmization by Guido d'Arezzo (A.D. 980–1050) and its development into modern syllable systems may be found in music history books, encyclopedias, or dictionaries.

EXERCISE 8.1

Playing major scales on the keyboard

Using the example as a guide, (1) indicate by arrows and by numbers 1–8 the keys on the keyboard required to produce the sound of the scale, (2) indicate whole steps and half steps, (3) then play the scale ascending for one octave.

Example: D Major

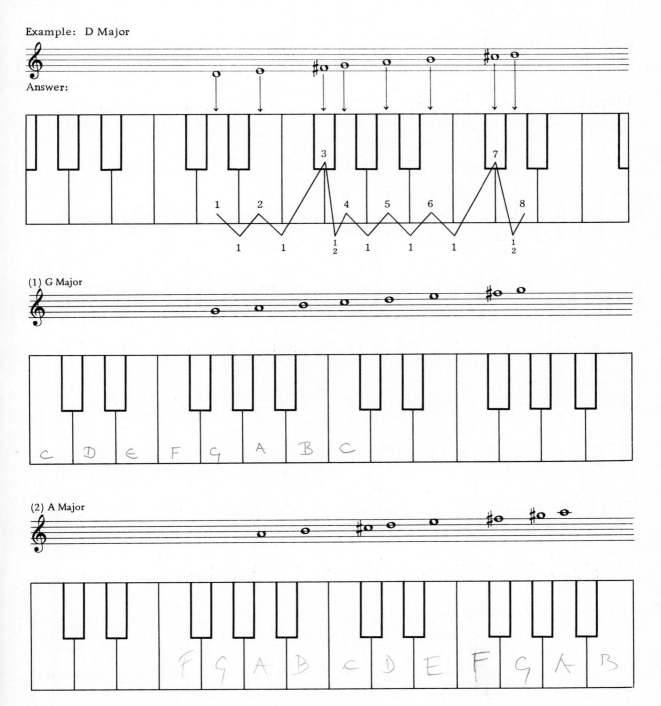

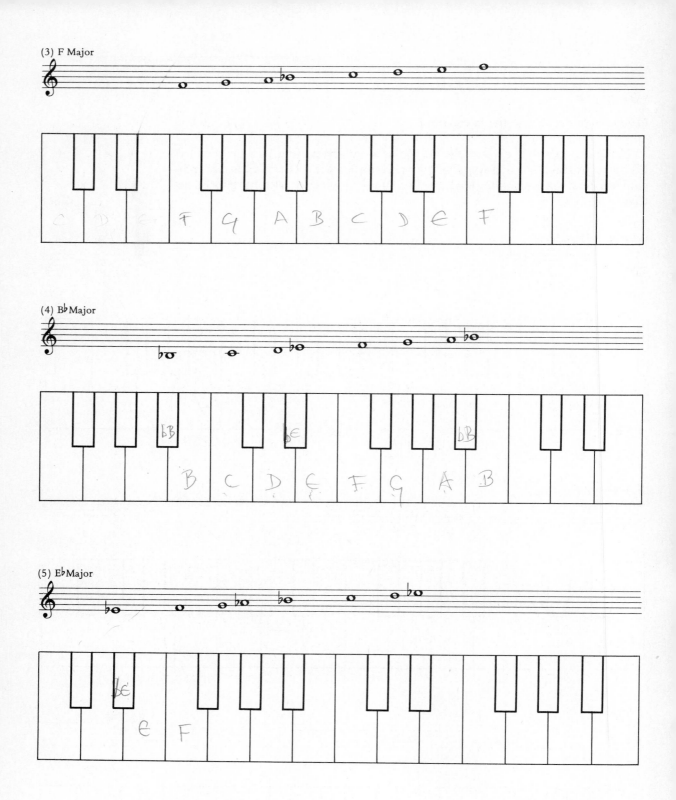

EXERCISE 8.2

Playing major scales on the keyboard

This exercise is similar to Exercise 8.1 although it does not show the staff. Number the keys, indicate whole steps and half steps, then play.

(1) E Major

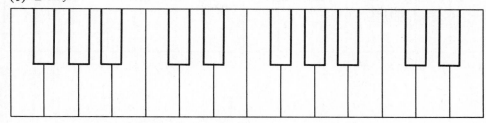

(2) B Major

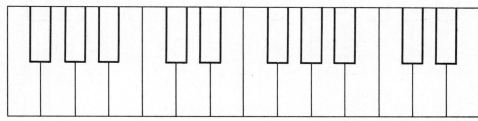

(3) F# Major

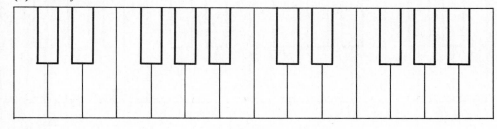

(4) C# Major

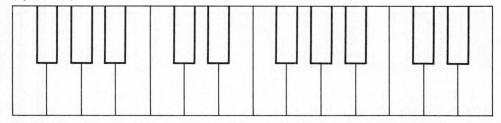

(5) A♭ Major

(6) D♭ Major

(7) G♭ Major

(8) C♭ Major

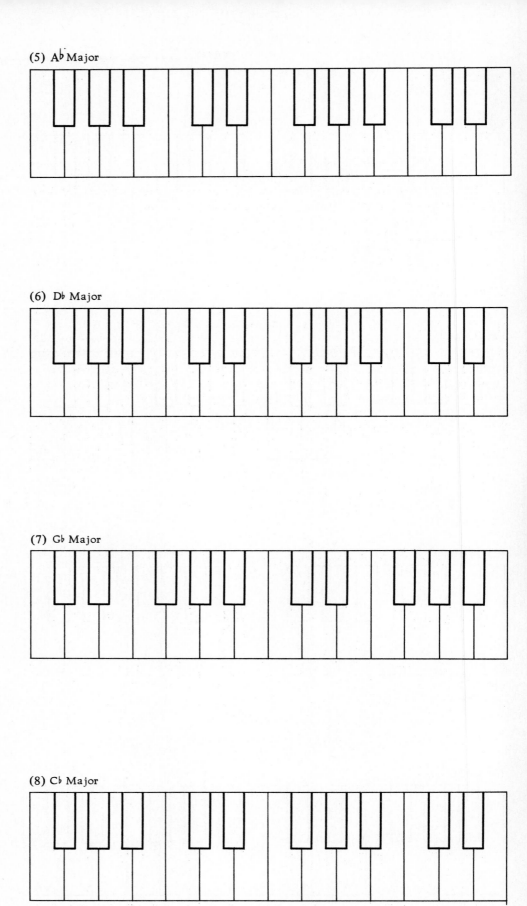

EXERCISE 8.3

Playing all major scales at the keyboard

Play any of the 15 major scales. Spell each scale as you play it. Be sure that each interval is the correct whole step or half step. Play *both* ascending and descending for one octave. You may refer to the scales you wrote in Exercise 4.1. Practice until you can play without looking at the music.

(*Return* to page 77)

EXERCISE 8.4

Singing major scales

Choose any single pitch which can be used as the tonic tone of a major scale. Sing the scale in three ways: (1) by numbers, (2) by letter names and (3) by syllables, as shown in Figures 8.5–7. Sing each of the fifteen major scales in this manner. You may sing these from the scales you wrote in Exercise 4.1. If necessary, play the scale as you sing until you feel able to sing without the piano. Use the piano at any time to check your accuracy.

(To continue the study of **Pitch,** *go directly* to **Chapter 10,** page 97)

CHAPTER NINE

Time
(continued)

Notation of the Simple Beat
Simple Meter (Time) Signatures
Notation of the Compound Beat
Compound Meter Signatures

We have found that beats in music can be grouped in twos, threes, and fours, and that they can also be divided into two or three equal parts. We have experienced these sensations and depicted them on paper with six meter designations and diagrams, previously shown in Figures 7.3 and 7.4. Most music is written in these six metrical patterns, but each pattern can be represented on paper only when a note value is assigned to the beat. We shall first study how a note value may be assigned to represent the simple beat, or *notation of the simple beat,* followed by a similar study of the *notation of the compound beat.*

Notation of the Simple Beat

A simple beat divides into two equal parts. Therefore, a note assigned to represent a simple beat must have a value divisible by two. The value most often used by composers to represent the simple beat is the quarter note.[1]

FIGURE 9.1 *Note Values Assigned to Represent the Simple Beat.*

The quarter note may represent the simple beat:

beat

♩ = 1/4 value

♫ = simple division

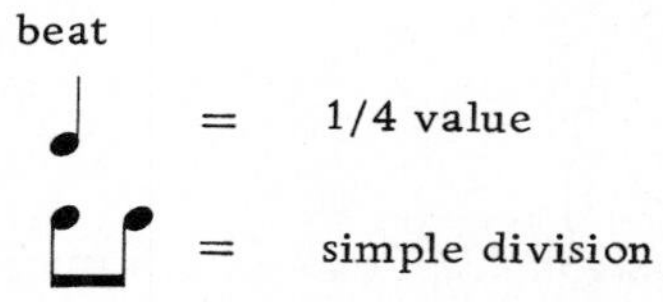

1. Theoretically, any note value divisible by two could represent a simple beat. For the present, we shall study three different note values, the quarter, the eighth and the half, which are commonly used to represent the simple beat.

The eighth note may also represent the simple beat:

beat

♪   =   1/8 value

♫   =   simple division

The half note may represent the simple beat:

beat

𝅗𝅥   =   1/2 value

♩ ♩   =   simple division

When we know the number of beats in a group and the assigned value of a beat, we can derive a *meter signature*.[2]

Simple Meter (Time) Signatures

A meter signature is a pair of numbers aligned vertically, such as $\frac{2}{4}$, $\frac{4}{8}$, etc., and placed at the beginning of a composition. It may be compared to a mathematical fraction placed on the staff with the numerator above and denominator below the third line. Its function is to indicate to the performer (1) which metrical pattern is to be used within each measure and in the piece of music as a whole, and (2) what note values will be used to represent the metrical pattern. Simple meter signature is derived according to the beat value and the beat grouping as shown in Figure 9.2.

Observe in Figure 9.2 that all meter signatures with the numerator of 2 indicate duple simple meter; all with the numerator of 3 indicate triple simple meter; and all with the numerator 4 indicate quadruple meter. The denominator 8 means that the eighth note value (♪) represents one beat; the denominator 4 means that the quarter note value (♩) represents one beat; the denominator 2 means that the half note value (𝅗𝅥) represents the beat; etc. Figure 9.3 shows the meaning of different simple meter signatures by illustrating the notation of their metrical patterns.

2. Frequently called *time signature*. From a mathematical point of view, a time signature shows merely the total number of note values in a measure. From the viewpoint of traditional practice, the signature also provides insight into the organization of durations within the measure. For this reason, the term *meter signature*, denoting a scheme of note values and pulses, is commonly found in theoretical writings. Notwithstanding, the terms may be used interchangeably.

FIGURE 9.2 *Derivation of Simple Meter (Time) Signatures.*

Beat Value	Beat Grouping (per measure)		Meter (Time) Signature	Meter Name
$\frac{1}{8}$	one $\frac{1}{8}$ $+$	two $\frac{1}{8}$ $=$	$\frac{2}{8}$	
$\frac{1}{4}$	one $\frac{1}{4}$ $+$	two $\frac{1}{4}$ $=$	$\frac{2}{4}$	DUPLE SIMPLE
$\frac{1}{2}$	one $\frac{1}{2}$ $+$	two $\frac{1}{2}$ $=$	$\frac{2}{2}$ or $\mathbb{C}$*	
$\frac{1}{8}$	one $\frac{1}{8}$ $+$ two $\frac{1}{8}$ $+$	three $\frac{1}{8}$ $=$	$\frac{3}{8}$	
$\frac{1}{4}$	one $\frac{1}{4}$ $+$ two $\frac{1}{4}$ $+$	three $\frac{1}{4}$ $=$	$\frac{3}{4}$	TRIPLE SIMPLE
$\frac{1}{2}$	one $\frac{1}{2}$ $+$ two $\frac{1}{2}$ $+$	three $\frac{1}{2}$ $=$	$\frac{3}{2}$	
$\frac{1}{8}$	one $\frac{1}{8}$ $+$ two $\frac{1}{8}$ $+$ three $\frac{1}{8}$ $+$	four $\frac{1}{8}$ $=$	$\frac{4}{8}$	
$\frac{1}{4}$	one $\frac{1}{4}$ $+$ two $\frac{1}{4}$ $+$ three $\frac{1}{4}$ $+$	four $\frac{1}{4}$ $=$	$\frac{4}{4}$ or $\mathbf{C}$**	QUADRUPLE SIMPLE
$\frac{1}{2}$	one $\frac{1}{2}$ $+$ two $\frac{1}{2}$ $+$ three $\frac{1}{2}$ $+$	four $\frac{1}{2}$ $=$	$\frac{4}{2}$	

* called *cut time:* $\mathbb{C}$ is a symbol substituting for 2/2.
** called *common time;* C is a symbol substituting for 4/4.

87

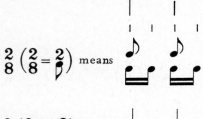

Numerator 2: Duple Metrical Pattern

$\frac{2}{8}\left(\frac{2}{8}=\frac{2}{♪}\right)$ means

two beats per measure, the eighth note represents the beat; each beat divides into two sixteenth notes

$\frac{2}{4}\left(\frac{2}{4}=\frac{2}{♩}\right)$ means

two beats per measure, the quarter note represents the beat; each beat divides into two eighth notes

$\frac{2}{2}\left(\frac{2}{2}=\frac{2}{𝅗𝅥}\right)$ means

two beats per measure, the half note represents the beat; each beat divides into two quarter notes

FIGURE 9.3 *Meaning of Simple Meter Signatures.*

Numerator 3: Triple Simple Metrical Pattern

$\frac{3}{8}\left(\frac{3}{8}=\frac{3}{♪}\right)$ means

three beats per measure, the eighth note represents the beat; each beat divides into two sixteenth notes

$\frac{3}{4}\left(\frac{3}{4}=\frac{3}{♩}\right)$ means

three beats per measure, the quarter note represents the beat; each beat divides into two eighth notes

$\frac{3}{2}\left(\frac{3}{2}=\frac{3}{𝅗𝅥}\right)$ means

three beats per measure, the half note represents the beat; each beat divides into two quarter notes

Numerator 4: Quadruple Simple Metrical Pattern

$\frac{4}{8}\left(\frac{4}{8}=\frac{4}{♪}\right)$ means

four beats per measure, the eighth note represents the beat; each beat divides into two sixteenth notes

$\frac{4}{4}\left(\frac{4}{4}=\frac{4}{♩}\right)$ means

four beats per measure, the quarter note represents the beat; each beat divides into two eighth notes

$\frac{4}{2}\left(\frac{4}{2}=\frac{4}{𝅗𝅥}\right)$ means

four beats per measure, the half note represents the beat; each beat divides into two quarter notes

EXERCISES
9.1, 9.2

Notation of the Compound Beat

A compound beat divides into three equal parts. Therefore a note representing a compound beat must have a value divisible by three. Such a value requires a *dotted note*. A dot placed after a note (♩·) increases the duration by one half of the value of the note. The value most often used by composers to represent the compound beat is the dotted quarter note.[3]

FIGURE 9.4 *Note Values Assigned to Represent the Compound Beat.*

The dotted quarter note may represent the compound beat:

beat

$$♩. = ♩ + ♪ \quad \text{therefore} \quad ♩. = 3/8 \text{ value}$$
$$\tfrac{1}{4} + \tfrac{1}{8} \qquad \qquad ♫♪ = \text{compound division}$$
$$\left(\tfrac{2}{8} + \tfrac{1}{8} = \tfrac{3}{8}\right)$$

The dotted eighth note also may be used to represent the compound beat:

beat

$$♪. = ♪ + ♬ \quad \text{therefore} \quad ♪. = \quad 3/16 \text{ value}$$
$$\tfrac{1}{8} + \tfrac{1}{16} \qquad \qquad ♬♬ = \text{compound division}$$
$$\left(\tfrac{2}{16} + \tfrac{1}{16} = \tfrac{3}{16}\right)$$

The dotted half note may be used to represent the compound beat:

beat

$$\textstyle𝅗𝅥. = 𝅗𝅥 + ♩ \quad \text{therefore} \quad 𝅗𝅥. = \quad 3/4 \text{ value}$$
$$\tfrac{1}{2} + \tfrac{1}{4} \qquad \qquad ♩♩♩ = \text{compound division}$$
$$\left(\tfrac{2}{4} + \tfrac{1}{4} = \tfrac{3}{4}\right)$$

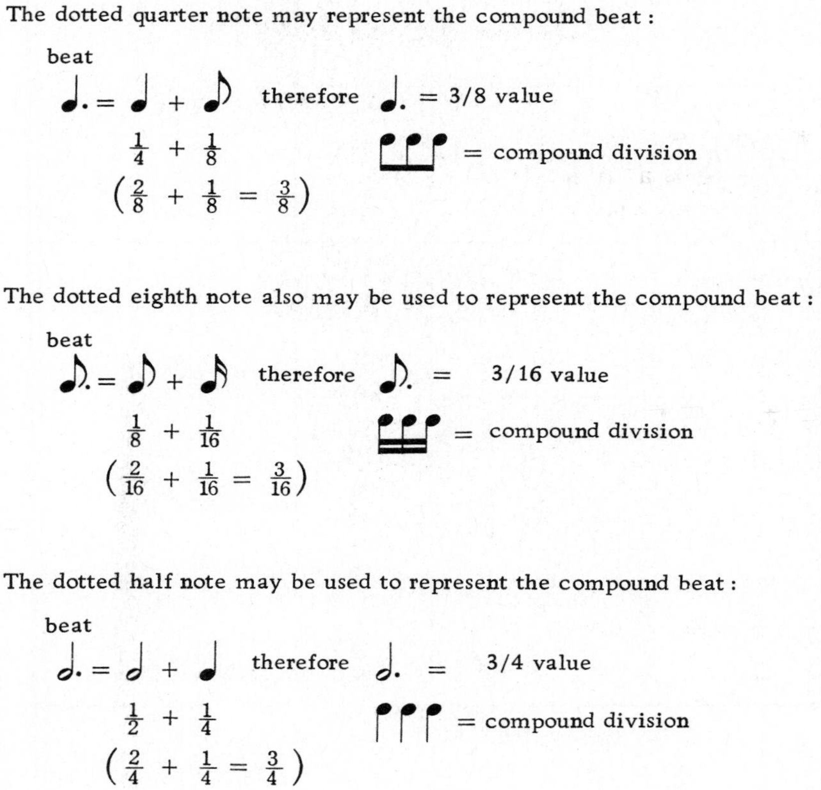

Notice that a dotted quarter can be represented mathematically only by the fraction ⅜; the dotted eighth only by the fraction ³⁄₁₆; and the dotted half note only by the fraction ¾.

From the number of beats in a group and the assigned value of a beat, we can derive the *compound meter signatures*.

Compound Meter Signatures

The compound meter signature is derived from the beat value and the beat grouping as shown in Figure 9.5.

3. Theoretically, any note value divisible by three could represent a compound beat. For the present, we shall study three values, the dotted quarter, the dotted eighth, and the dotted half, which are note values commonly used to represent the compound beat.

FIGURE 9.5 *Derivation of Compound Meter Signatures.*

Beat Value	Beat Grouping (per measure)				Meter (Time) Signature	Meter Name
$\frac{3}{16}$	one $\frac{3}{16}$	+	two $\frac{3}{16}$	=	$\frac{6}{16}$	
$\frac{3}{8}$	one $\frac{3}{8}$	+	two $\frac{3}{8}$	=	$\frac{6}{8}$	DUPLE COMPOUND
$\frac{3}{4}$	one $\frac{3}{4}$	+	two $\frac{3}{4}$	=	$\frac{6}{4}$	
$\frac{3}{16}$	one $\frac{3}{16}$ + two $\frac{3}{16}$ + three $\frac{3}{16}$			=	$\frac{9}{16}$	
$\frac{3}{8}$	one $\frac{3}{8}$ + two $\frac{3}{8}$ + three $\frac{3}{8}$			=	$\frac{9}{8}$	TRIPLE COMPOUND
$\frac{3}{4}$	one $\frac{3}{4}$ + two $\frac{3}{4}$ + three $\frac{3}{4}$			=	$\frac{9}{4}$	
$\frac{3}{16}$	one $\frac{3}{16}$ + two $\frac{3}{16}$ + three $\frac{3}{16}$ + four $\frac{3}{16}$			=	$\frac{12}{16}$	
$\frac{3}{8}$	one $\frac{3}{8}$ + two $\frac{3}{8}$ + three $\frac{3}{8}$ + four $\frac{3}{8}$			=	$\frac{12}{8}$	QUADRUPLE COMPOUND
$\frac{3}{4}$	one $\frac{3}{4}$ + two $\frac{3}{4}$ + three $\frac{3}{4}$ + four $\frac{3}{4}$			=	$\frac{12}{4}$	

Observe in Figure 9.5 that all meter signatures with the numerator of 6 indicate duple compound meter; all with the numerator of 9 indicate triple compound meter; and all with the numerator 12 indicate quadruple compound meter. Unlike the simple meter signature where the numerator is identical with the number of beats in a group, in a compound meter signature the numerator is identical with the number of divisions of the beats. The denominator shows the assigned value to each division of the compound beat, three of which equal one beat. Figure 9.6 shows the meaning of different compound meter signatures by illustrating the notation of their metrical patterns. Signatures in Figure 9.6 such as $\frac{2}{\beta\cdot}$, though used by only a few composers, make the meaning of compound signatures much more clear.

FIGURE 9.6 *Meaning of Compound Meter Signatures.*

Numerator 6: Duple Compound Metrical Pattern

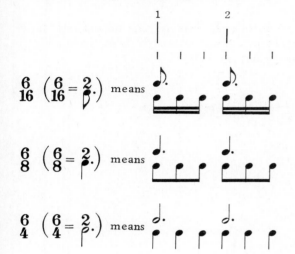

$\frac{6}{16}$ $\left(\frac{6}{16}=\frac{2}{\beta\cdot}\right)$ means

two beats per measure, the dotted eighth note represents the beat; each beat divides into three sixteenth notes

$\frac{6}{8}$ $\left(\frac{6}{8}=\frac{2}{\beta\cdot}\right)$ means

two beats per measure, the dotted quarter note represents the beat; each beat divides into three eighth notes

$\frac{6}{4}$ $\left(\frac{6}{4}=\frac{2}{\beta\cdot}\right)$ means

two beats per measure, the dotted half note represents the beat; each beat divides into three quarter notes

Numerator 9: Triple Compound Metrical Pattern

$\frac{9}{16}$ $\left(\frac{9}{16}=\frac{3}{\beta\cdot}\right)$ means

three beats per measure, the dotted eighth note represents the beat; each beat divides into three sixteenth notes

$\frac{9}{8}$ $\left(\frac{9}{8}=\frac{3}{\beta\cdot}\right)$ means

three beats per measure, the dotted quarter note represents the beat; each beat divides into three eighth notes

$\frac{9}{4}$ $\left(\frac{9}{4}=\frac{3}{\beta\cdot}\right)$ means

three beats per measure, the dotted half note represents the beat; each beat divides into three quarter notes

Numerator 12: Quadruple Compound Metrical Pattern

$\frac{12}{16}$ $\left(\frac{12}{16} = \frac{4}{\text{♪.}}\right)$ means ♪. ♪. ♪. ♪. four beats per measure, the dotted eighth note represents the beat; each beat divides into three sixteenth notes

$\frac{12}{8}$ $\left(\frac{12}{8} = \frac{4}{\text{♩.}}\right)$ means ♩. ♩. ♩. ♩. four beats per measure, the dotted quarter note represents the beat; each beat divides into three eighth notes

$\frac{12}{4}$ $\left(\frac{12}{4} = \frac{4}{\text{𝅗𝅥.}}\right)$ means 𝅗𝅥. 𝅗𝅥. 𝅗𝅥. 𝅗𝅥. four beats per measure, the dotted half note represents the beat; each beat divides into three quarter notes

EXERCISES
9.3, 9.4

EXERCISE 9.1

Identifying the metrical grouping in simple time

Place a meter signature before the given notation and name the meter in the blanks provided.

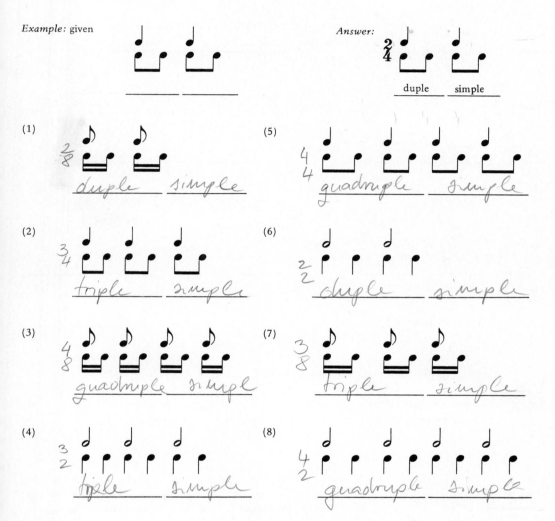

Example: given _____   _____

Answer: $\frac{2}{4}$ duple   simple

(1) $\frac{2}{8}$ *duple* *simple*

(5) $\frac{4}{4}$ *quadruple* *simple*

(2) $\frac{3}{4}$ *triple* *simple*

(6) $\frac{2}{2}$ *duple* *simple*

(3) $\frac{4}{8}$ *quadruple* *simple*

(7) $\frac{3}{8}$ *triple* *simple*

(4) $\frac{3}{2}$ *triple* *simple*

(8) $\frac{4}{2}$ *quadruple* *simple*

EXERCISE 9.2

Supplying metrical patterns for given simple time signatures

After the given time signature, write the metrical pattern using correct notation and name the meter.

Example: given $\frac{2}{4}$ *Answer:* $\frac{2}{4}$

_____   _____   duple simple

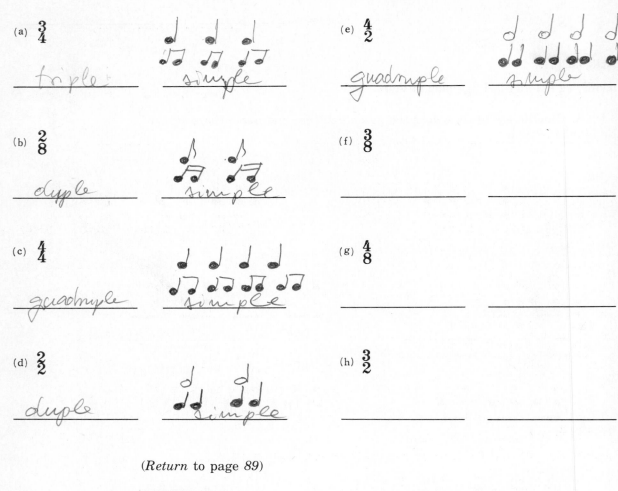

(a) $\frac{3}{4}$ triple   simple

(e) $\frac{4}{2}$ quadruple   simple

(b) $\frac{2}{8}$ duple   simple

(f) $\frac{3}{8}$

(c) $\frac{4}{4}$ quadruple   simple

(g) $\frac{4}{8}$

(d) $\frac{2}{2}$ duple   simple

(h) $\frac{3}{2}$

(*Return* to page *89*)

EXERCISE 9.3

Identifying the metrical grouping in compound time

Place a meter signature before the given notation and name the meter in the blanks provided, as done in Exercise 9.1.

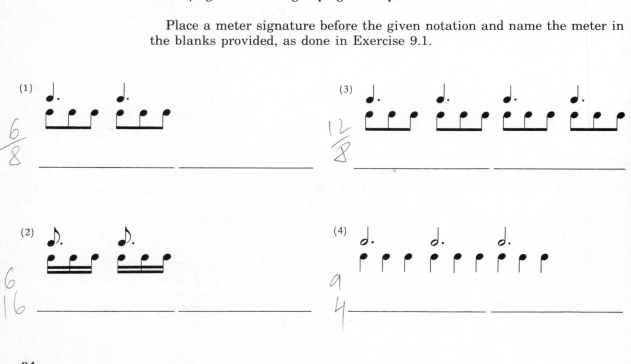

(1) $\frac{6}{8}$

(3) $\frac{12}{8}$

(2) $\frac{6}{16}$

(4) $\frac{9}{4}$

94

(5)

$\frac{6}{4}$

_____ _____

(8)

$\frac{12}{4}$

_____ _____

(6)

$\frac{9}{16}$

_____ _____

(9)

$\frac{12}{16}$

_____ _____

(7)

$\frac{9}{8}$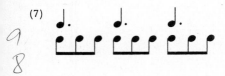

_____ _____

EXERCISE 9.4

Supplying metrical patterns for given compound time signatures

Follow directions given in Exercise 9.2.

(1) $\frac{6}{8}$

_____ _____

(4) $\frac{9}{4}$

_____ _____

(2) $\frac{12}{4}$

_____ _____

(5) $\frac{9}{16}$

_____ _____

(3) $\frac{9}{8}$

_____ _____

(6) $\frac{6}{4}$

_____ _____

(7) $\frac{12}{8}$

(9) $\frac{12}{16}$

(8) $\frac{6}{16}$

(To continue the study of **Time,** *go directly* to **Chapter 11,** page *111*)

CHAPTER TEN

Pitch: Major Key Signatures

Key
Key Signature
Circle of Fifths
Key Signatures on the Staff

The major scale, with its characteristic locations of half steps and whole steps, constitutes a musical pattern having its own unique aural quality. We have found that the major scale pattern can be written with fifteen different locations (letter names) as tonic, with each location other than that of C requiring a varying number of sharps or flats to maintain the correct half step and whole step relationships. Since each of these fifteen scales has the same characteristic sound, there are not really fifteen different scales; there is simply *one* major scale structure which can be written or played at fifteen different locations.

Much music commonly performed today (including most music of the 17th–19th centuries) is based on either one of two scale patterns: the major scale as already studied, and the minor scale, to be studied in Chapter 13. Music is said to be in *major* when the pitches used can be arranged in alphabetical order with a resulting major scale pattern. In "Joy to the World" (George F. Handel, 1685–1759), the first line of the melody already assumes the pattern of the D major scale.[1]

FIGURE 10.1   *"Joy to the World," D Major Scale.*

In the folksong in Figure 10.2, we find the same tones in a different order, but still resulting in the same D major scale.

1. Figures 10.1 and 10.2 include all members of the major scale. Many melodies do not include all scale tones, but enough are present to make the scale easily discernible, for example, the melody *Auld Lang Syne* (see page 53).

FIGURE 10.2 *Folksong, D Major Scale.*

Both of these tunes are said to be in *major* because they are based on the construction of the major scale.

It is possible to begin "Joy to the World" on a different note, with a resulting change in scale spelling.

FIGURE 10.3 *"Joy to the World," Bb Major Scale.*

We also can write the folksong in Figure 10.2 based on any other major scale. In Figure 10.4 the scale is built on a tonic of F♯.

FIGURE 10.4 *Folksong, F♯ Major Scale.*

It is easy to see that each of these tunes could be written using any of the fifteen major scale locations. We could identify a piece of music by saying it uses a certain scale, but instead, we say the music is in a certain *key*.

Key

The term *key* refers to the letter name of the tonic (first degree) of that scale upon which the composition is based. The letter name of the tonic is also called *keynote*. Figures 10.1 and 10.2 are therefore in the *key* of D major because each uses a major scale with the tonic, or keynote, of D. In similar manner we would identify "Joy to the World" in Figure 10.3 as being in the key of Bb major, and the folksong in Figure 10.4 as being in the key of F♯ major.

Music could be written with the correct accidentals placed before each note where needed, as in the preceding figures, but this is obviously cumbersome and makes the music appear unduly complicated. To facilitate the notation of accidentals we use a device called *key signature*.

Key Signature

The *key signature* is a group of accidentals found on the staff at the beginning of a composition. This group consists of the accidentals used in the scale of the composition. When the music uses a major or minor scale, the signature can also be used to identify the key of the composition. If we rewrite Figure 10.4 by placing the sharps in a certain order at the beginning of the staff, we find we have a key signature of six sharps, which, as we will learn, will designate the key of F♯ major. The key signature is placed before the time signature.

FIGURE 10.5 *Folksong, Key Signature for F♯ Major.*

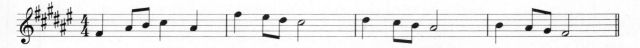

By extracting the accidentals from each major scale in this way, we can find the number and names of sharps or flats for each major key, and the key signature for each. Including C (no sharps and no flats), there are fifteen major keys, just as there are fifteen locations of the major scale.

FIGURE 10.6 *Number and Names of Accidentals for Major Key Signatures.*

Name of key (Name of tonic or keynote)	Number of #'s or ♭'s in key signature	Names of #'s or ♭'s						
C	none							
G	1♯	f♯						
D	2♯	f♯,	c♯					
A	3♯	f♯,	c♯,	g♯				
E	4♯	f♯,	c♯,	g♯,	d♯			
B	5♯	f♯,	c♯,	g♯,	d♯,	a♯		
F♯	6♯	f♯,	c♯,	g♯,	d♯,	a♯,	e♯	
C♯	7♯	f♯,	c♯,	g♯,	d♯,	a♯,	e♯,	b♯
(C)	(none)							
F	1♭	b♭						
B♭	2♭	b♭,	e♭					
E♭	3♭	b♭,	e♭,	a♭				
A♭	4♭	b♭,	e♭,	a♭,	d♭			
D♭	5♭	b♭,	e♭,	a♭,	d♭,	g♭		
G♭	6♭	b♭,	e♭,	a♭,	d♭,	g♭,	c♭	
C♭	7♭	b♭,	e♭,	a♭,	d♭,	g♭,	c♭,	f♭,

A common way of illustrating the order of key signatures, with the numbers of accidentals in each, is through the *circle of fifths*.

Circle of Fifths

To understand the *circle of fifths,* the student must first be able to measure the interval of a perfect fifth.[2] A perfect fifth spans five staff degrees and is comprised of three whole steps and one half step, or seven half steps. However, a perfect fifth can be quickly calculated without counting steps by using information already learned in connection with the scale. Consider the note from which the measurement is to be made as tonic. From a tonic note up to its dominant note is an ascending perfect fifth.

FIGURE 10.7 *Ascending Perfect Fifths.*

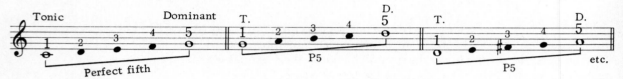

From a tonic note down to its subdominant note is a descending perfect fifth.

FIGURE 10.8 *Descending Perfect Fifths.*

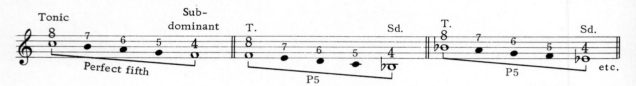

It is through the interval of the perfect fifth that keys are related to each other, as shown in Figures 10.6 and 10.9. Starting with C, we count *up* a perfect fifth to find the keynote (G) for the scale with *one* sharp; we count up a perfect fifth from G to find the keynote (D) for the scale with *two* sharps, and so

FIGURE 10.9 *Progressions by Fifths from C.*

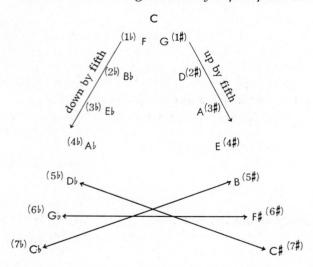

2. Interval names, including other kinds of fifths, will be studied in Chapters 17 and 18.

on until we reach C♯ with *seven* sharps. The flat keys are related in a similar manner. Starting with C, we count *down* a perfect fifth to find the keynote (F) for the scale with *one* flat; we count down a perfect fifth from F to find the keynote (B♭) for the scale of *two* flats, and so on until we reach C♭ with *seven* flats. This process is diagrammed in Figure 10.9, where it can be seen that each progression up by a fifth adds one new sharp, and each progression down by a fifth adds one new flat.

Further observation of Figure 10.9 shows that the key names used for 5, 6, and 7 sharps have enharmonic equivalents in the names for keys of 5, 6, and 7 flats: B (5 sharps) and C♭ (7 flats); F♯ (6 sharps) and G♭ (6 flats); C♯ (7 sharps) and D♭ (5 flats). By reconstructing Figure 10.9 so that these enharmonic keys coincide, the *circle of fifths* for major keys is produced.

FIGURE 10.10   *Circle of Fifths for Major Keys.*

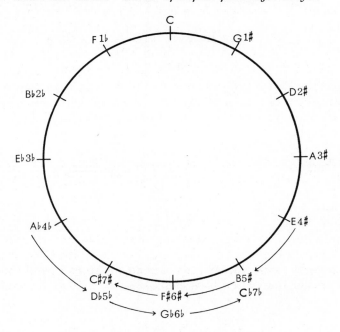

This circle includes all the major key names with the sharp keys reading clockwise from C, and the flat keys reading counterclockwise from C. The circle is joined by the three enharmonic keys. The number of sharps or flats for each key can be determined by counting the number of fifths away from C. For example, A has 3 sharps because it is the third key clockwise from C; D♭ has 5 flats because it is five keys counterclockwise from C.

Now that we have studied the names of major keys and the number of accidentals for each, we are ready to learn the traditional placement of sharps and flats for *key signatures on the staff.*

EXERCISES 10.1, 10.2, 10.3, 10.4, 10.5

Key Signatures on the Staff

Accidentals of key signatures (listed in Figure 10.6) are positioned on the staff in a certain way. For sharp keys, the first sharp (F♯) appears on the fifth line of the treble clef, and on the fourth line of the bass clef.[3]

3. Actually, accidentals or notes are placed on a staff, not on a clef. To say, "accidentals or notes on treble or bass clef," is simply a common manner of speaking.

This sharp applies to any F in the musical composition whether on the same line or in any other location, and this principle is observed for any other sharps (or flats) of the key signature. All sharps are placed as shown in Figure 10.11.

FIGURE 10.11 *C Major and Sharp Key Signatures.*

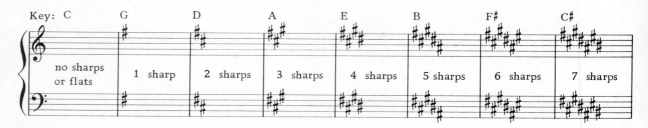

Notice that the sharps progress from left to right in an orderly arrangement and that the *pattern* of accidentals in key signatures is the same for treble and bass, the up-and-down contour changed only at sharps 4 and 5.

For flat keys, the first flat (B♭) appears on the third line of the treble clef, and on the second line of the bass clef.

All flats are placed as shown in Figure 10.12.

FIGURE 10.12 *C Major and Flat Key Signatures.*

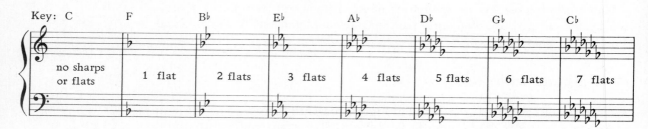

Notice that the flats progress from left to right in an orderly and regular arrangement and that the *pattern* of accidentals in key signatures is the same for treble and bass.

Attention to the preceding study will prevent your making these common errors:

For quick identification of a major key in a signature of sharps, the keynote occupies the staff degree immediately above the last sharp. Try this method in Figure 10.11.

For quick identification of a major key in a signature of two or more flats, the keynote is identical with the penultimate (next to last) flat. Try this method in Figure 10.12.

EXERCISES
10.6, 10.7

EXERCISE 10.1

**Writing the numbers of accidentals
for keys on the circle of fifths**

On the circle of fifths below, the key names are given. Beside each key name
write the correct number of sharps or flats. The answer for G major is given.

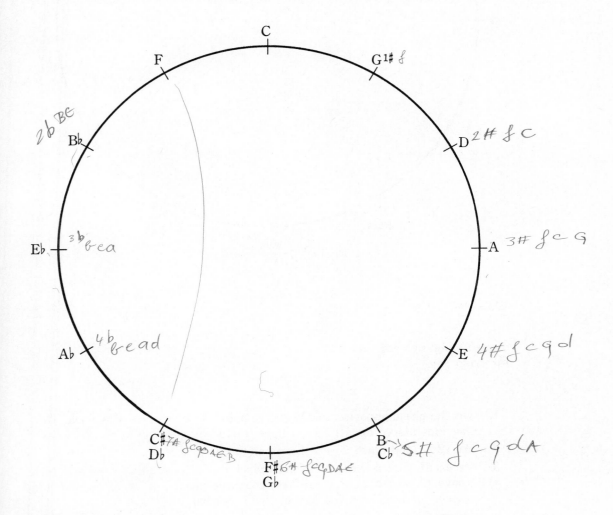

EXERCISE 10.2

Writing names of keys on the circle of fifths

On the circle below, the numbers of accidentals for key signatures are given.
Beside each, write the name of the major key. The answer for one flat is given.

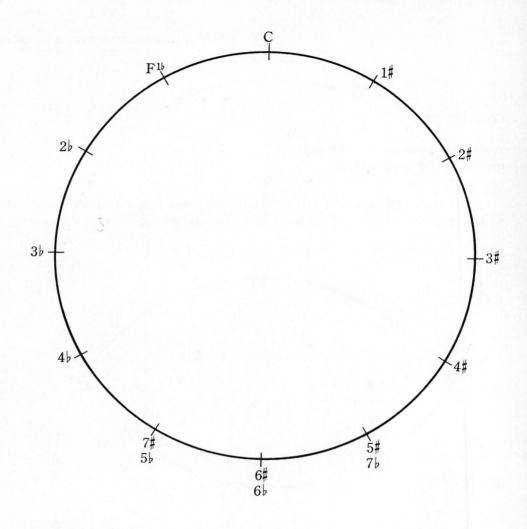

EXERCISE 10.3

**Constructing the circle of fifths
for major keys**

1. On the circle opposite, mark twelve points like the face of a clock. This provides places for all fifteen keys, including three enharmonic keys.
2. At 12 o'clock place C (no sharps or flats).
3. Proceeding clockwise, at 1 o'clock place the letter name of the key a fifth above C, which is G (1 sharp); continue clockwise in fifths and add sharps, ending with the key of C♯ (7 sharps).
4. Proceeding counterclockwise, at 11 o'clock place the letter name of the key a fifth below C, which is F (1 flat); continue counterclockwise in fifths and add flats, ending with the key of C♭ (7 flats).

With practice, you should be able to demonstrate the circle (from memory) on paper or at the board in *one minute*. Compare your results with Figure 10.10.

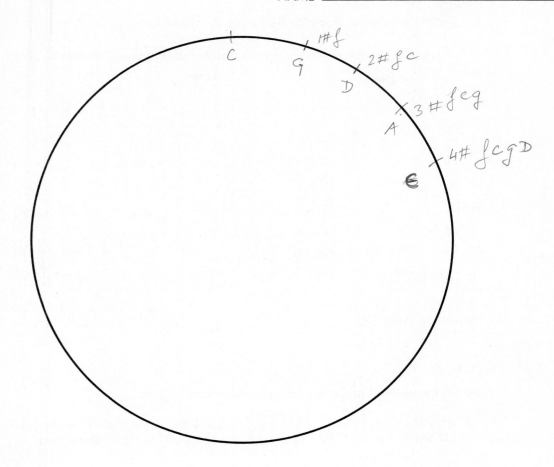

EXERCISE 10.4

Identifying major key names from the number of accidentals

In each blank space, write the correct major key name according to the number of sharps or flats given.

(1) 2♯   __D__   (D♭ = 5♭)   (8) 7♯   C♯ (C = 0)

(2) 4♭   __A♭__   (A = 3♯)   (9) 6♭   G♭ (G = 1♯)

(3) 3♭   __E♭__   (E = 4♯)   (10) 5♭   D♭ (D = 2♯)

(4) 5♯   __B__   (B♭ = 2♭)   (11) 4♯   E (E♭ = 3♭)

(5) 1♯   __G__   (G♭ = 6♭)   (12) 1♭   F (F♯ = 6♯)

(6) 7♭   __C♭__   (C = 0)   (13) 6♯   F♯ (F = 1♭)

(7) 3♯   __A__   (A♭ = 4♭)   (14) 2♭   B♭ (B = 5♯)

EXERCISE 10.5

Naming the number of sharps or flats when the major key is given

In each blank space, write the correct number of sharps or flats for the given major key.

(1) B♭   _2♭_   (8) G♭   _6♭_

(2) D♭   _5♭_   (9) E   _4#_

(3) A   _3#_   (10) F#   _6#_

(4) G   _1#_   (11) F   _1♭_

(5) C#   _7#_   (12) C♭   _7♭_

(6) E♭   _3♭_   (13) B   _5#_

(7) D   _2#_   (14) A♭   _4♭_

(*Return* to page *101*)

EXERCISE 10.6

Identifying name of major key when key signature is given

For each key signature (1) write the name of the major key below the staff, and (2) write the tonic note of the key on the staff, using a whole note.

Example:

Answer: ⟶ E major

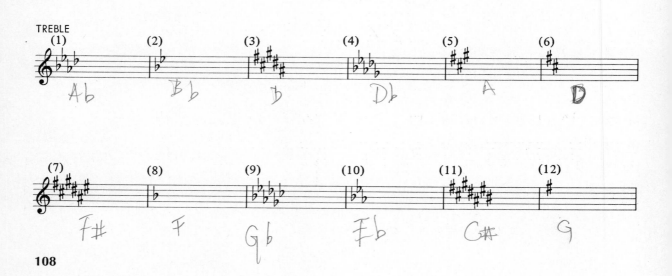

TREBLE

(1) A♭   (2) B♭   (3) D♭   (4) D♭   (5) A   (6) D

(7) F#   (8) F   (9) G♭   (10) E♭   (11) C#   (12) G

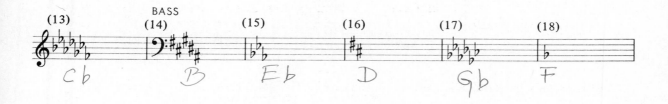

(13) Cb (14) BASS B (15) Eb (16) D (17) Gb (18) F

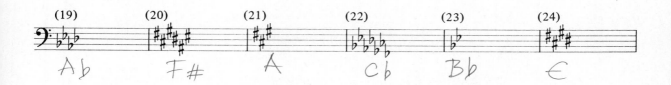

(19) Ab (20) F# (21) A (22) Cb (23) Bb (24) E

(25) C# (26) G (27) Db

EXERCISE 10.7

Writing major key signatures

Write the correct number of sharps or flats on the correct lines and spaces of the great staff for each given major key.

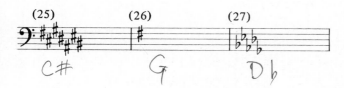

Example: given A major

Answer:

(1) G major (2) Eb major (3) C# major (4) Gb major

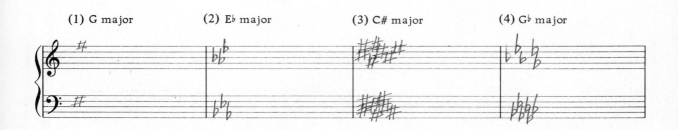

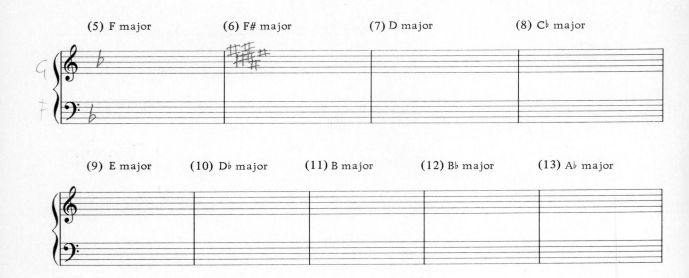

(5) F major   (6) F# major   (7) D major   (8) C♭ major

(9) E major   (10) D♭ major   (11) B major   (12) B♭ major   (13) A♭ major

(To continue the study of **Pitch,** *go directly* to **Chapter 13,** page *141*)

CHAPTER ELEVEN

Time
(continued)

Conductor's Beats
Rhythm
Anacrusis
Rhythmic Reading

With the knowledge gained thus far concerning pitch and time, it becomes possible to advance our skills in the reading of music. There are two stages of competence in the reading of music: the first in which the performer looks at a given note and reacts in some mechanical manner, such as depressing a key on the piano, or placing the finger on a violin string, and the second in which the performer looks at a given note and knows before playing it how that note will sound. For musicians, the ultimate goal is the accomplishment of the second stage. An important attribute of the accomplished musician is the ability to read music of varying complexities, from the single melodic line to the two staves of notation necessary for piano music, or even an orchestral score with a full page of staves representing all the instruments of the symphony orchestra. An effective approach to the desired skills of music reading is through practicing the technique of singing a melody at sight. Singing is preferable to performance at an instrument, because in singing it is impossible to fall back on any mechanical help (such as a key) to help locate a correct pitch.

In singing at sight (sightsinging) two kinds of reading are necessary: (1) reading note values and (2) reading pitches. We will begin by learning to read the durations of different note values. Most students have found that their study is made easier if they can actually feel the metrical grouping as they perform. This can be accomplished in a dramatic way by the use of *conductor's beats*.

Conductor's Beats

Conductor's beats are patterns of hand gestures used to indicate groupings of beats.[1] While the motions or diagrams of the beats may vary among conductors, certain basic movements are so standardized that they are accepted by musicians throughout the world.

1. Herman Scherchen (*Handbook of Conducting*, Oxford University Press, London, 1933) considers that there are three distinct purposes in conducting: (1) to present the metric course of the music; (2) to indicate its expressive, structural features; and (3) to actually guide the musicians—preventing faulty performance and correcting fluctuations or inequalities. In this present course of study, the student will be concerned only with the first purpose, to present the metric course of the music.

The following right-hand diagrams for conductor's beats are recommended because all beats occur approximately on the same horizontal plane. For the student seated in a classroom this horizontal plane might be at desk-top level, or, if standing, the horizontal plane is about waist high.

FIGURE 11.1 *Conductor's Beats.*[2]

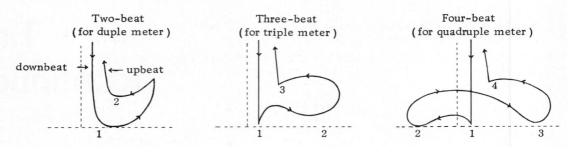

Two-beat (for duple meter) Three-beat (for triple meter) Four-beat (for quadruple meter)

EXERCISES
11.1, 11.2

The numbers indicate the place in the conductor's beat where each beat begins, just as tapping marks the beginning of each beat as practiced in Chapter 5. The first beat in all diagrams is called the *downbeat* and always coincides with the first beat of a measure. In any of these patterns, the last beat is described by an upward motion of the hand and is called an *upbeat*.

The two-beat can be used for duple simple meter signatures (numerator of 2) or duple compound signatures (numerator of 6). In the same way, the three-beat can be used for meter signatures with numerators of 3 or 9, and the four-beat for meter signatures with numerators of 4 or 12.

FIGURE 11.2 *Meter Signatures and Accompanying Conductor's Beats.*

	Meter Signatures						Accompanying Conductor's Beats
	Simple			Compound			
DUPLE	2/8	2/4	2/2 (¢)	6/16	6/8	6/4	TWO-BEAT
TRIPLE	3/8	3/4	3/2	9/16	9/8	9/4	THREE-BEAT
QUADRUPLE	4/8	4/4 (C)	4/2	12/16	12/8	12/4	FOUR-BEAT

EXERCISE
11.3

Use of the conductor's beats alone does not differentiate simple and compound meter. While conducting with the right hand, the difference can be demonstrated by tapping with the left hand. Two taps with the left hand for each of

2. In addition to two, three, and four, there are other beat-patterns for one, five, six, etc. The student can expect to study these other beat-diagrams in later theory or conducting courses.

the beats in the right hand will describe simple meters; three taps with the left hand for each of the beats in the right hand will describe compound meters.

Using the conductor's beat and tapping with the left hand simultaneously is basically the same procedure shown in Chapter 7 in the diagrams, Figure 7.4, and practiced in the exercises. The only difference is in the right hand, where the conductor's beat is substituted for the beat-tap.

EXERCISES
11.4, 11.5T,
11.6, 11.7T,
11.8T

In our exercises in listening to melodies, you have also noticed that the pitches are of various durations, some the same as the beat, some the same as the division, and still others of lengths different from the beat or division. This feature of musical composition is called *rhythm*.

Rhythm

The occurrence of a series of sounds of varying durations is known as *rhythm*. In our previous study, the regularly recurring beats of music were shown to designate meter. Now we shall see that varying durations comprise the rhythm of the music.

FIGURE 11.3   *Rhythm and Meter.*

Rhythm, the occurence of various note values, is revealed in the melody.

Meter is the regularly recurring pulsation of beats.

Observe that the melody in Figure 11.3 does not start on the first beat of a measure; it begins with an *anacrusis*.

Anacrusis

The *anacrusis* is that part of the music occurring before the downbeat of the first complete measure. It may be described as an incomplete measure before the first full measure, and it may consist of one, two, or several notes. When the anacrusis occurs on the last beat or fraction of the last beat before the first complete measure, it is often called the "upbeat" or "pick-up."

The anacrusis is usually written as an incomplete measure, in which case, its value and the note values found in the final measure are equal to one full measure. In Figure 11.3 the value of the anacrusis, ♪♪ , added to the value of the final measure, ♩, is equal to a full measure of $\frac{3}{4}$ meter.

EXERCISE
11.9

Having now defined meter and rhythm, and having recognized the factor of anacrusis, we will combine these in a practical application known as *Rhythmic Reading*.

Rhythmic Reading

Rhythmic Reading, or rhythmic recitation, is a process in music by which note durations only, not pitches, are expressed in vocal sounds. Rhythmic reading is based on these principles:

(1) Any note occurring on a beat is recited by the number of that beat.

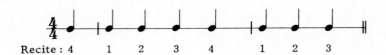

Recite : 4   1   2   3   4   1   2   3

(2) Any note, not recited by number, occurring on a fraction of a beat is recited by the syllable *ta* (tah).[3]

Recite: 1   2   3   ta   1   2   ta   3

also,

Recite: 1   2   ta   ta   1   ta   ta   2

(3) The syllable which originates with a note is held for the duration until the next appropriate syllable is articulated.[4]

Recite: 1 ———— ta   1 ———————— 2

also,

Recite: 1 ———— ta   ta   1   ta   2   1 ————

(4) At the occurrence of a rest, the reader remains silent.

EXERCISES
11.10, 11.11,
11.12, 11.13,
11.14

Recite: 1   2   3   ta 2 ta 3 ————   3

3. A variety of rhythmic syllables for beat division is used by different theorists and teachers, for example, $\frac{2}{4}$ ♫ ♫ *1 and 2 and* is a system widely used for younger students. Rhythmic reading of more complex music favors the use of a syllable beginning with the articulate sound of a consonant, such as *ta*, in place of the broad sound of *and*.

4. The *tie* is a curved line which connects two notes of the same pitch. The second note is not articulated and the result is a sustained unbroken sound equal to the duration of both notes.

EXERCISE 11.1

Drawing diagrams of conductor's beats

Draw right-hand diagrams and number the beats.
(a) Two-beat

(b) Three-beat

(c) Four-beat

EXERCISE 11.2

Practicing conductor's beats

Practice the two-, three-, and four-beats. Practice sometimes in front of a mirror. Have other students criticize your beats. Observe especially the clarity of your execution of the diagrams.

(*Return* to page *112*)

EXERCISE 11.3

Selecting the conductor's beat according to the meter signature

What conductor's beat would be used to accompany the following meter signatures?

Example: *Answer*:

$\frac{2}{8}$ two-beat

(1) $\frac{4}{4}$ _____   (10) $\frac{4}{2}$ _____

(2) $\frac{9}{8}$ _____   (11) $\frac{3}{4}$ _____

(3) $\frac{2}{2}$ _____   (12) $\frac{12}{16}$ _____

(4) $\frac{6}{8}$ _____   (13) $\frac{6}{4}$ _____

(5) $\frac{12}{4}$ _____   (14) $\frac{12}{8}$ _____

(6) $\frac{2}{4}$ _____   (15) $\frac{9}{16}$ _____

(7) $\frac{6}{16}$ _____   (16) $\frac{4}{8}$ _____

(8) $\frac{9}{4}$ _____   (17) $\frac{3}{2}$ _____

(9) $\frac{3}{8}$ _____

(*Return* to page *112*)

EXERCISE 11.4

Conducting and tapping simple meters (without music)

While conducting two (duple), three (triple), or four (quadruple), tap the simple division of the beat (division of two) with the other hand. The student can practice alone and outside of class. Ordinarily, this exercise requires much repetitious practice before the student feels at ease.

EXERCISE 11.5T

Conducting and tapping simple meters

The instructor will designate a melody from Exercise 7.2T. Observe the meter signature, make the appropriate conductor's beat, and tap the simple background in the left hand. As you continue conducting, the instructor will play the given melody. Observe that not all melodies start on the downbeat: some may start on other beats of the measure, or on the second division of the beat.

EXERCISE 11.6

Conducting and tapping compound meters (without music)

While conducting two, three, or four, tap the compound division of the beat (division of three) with the other hand. The student can practice alone and outside of class.

EXERCISE 11.7T

Conducting and tapping compound meters

The instructor will designate a melody from Exercise 7.4T. Observe the meter signature, make the appropriate conductor's beat, and tap the compound division in the left hand. Observe that the melody may begin on any beat, or on a division of a beat (if on a division of a beat, usually the third division). As you continue conducting, the instructor will play the melody.

EXERCISE 11.8T

Conducting and tapping simple or compound meters

Listen to a melody played by the instructor. Listen for meter (beat grouping and division) and location of downbeat. Conduct with the right hand and tap the division with the left hand. Use the music supplied for Exercise 7.5T. For additional material, use the following melodies from *Music for Sight Singing*. Observe the recommended metronome indications.

(1)	73	M.M. ♩ =	92	(9)	346	M.M. ♪. =	100
(2)	84	M.M. ♩ =	108	(10)	351	M.M. ♩. =	112
(3)	96	M.M. ♩ =	116	(11)	364	M.M. ♩ =	86
(4)	183	M.M. ♩. =	69	(12)	372	M.M. ♩. =	60
(5)	193	M.M. ♩. =	92	(13)	374	M.M. ♩. =	69
(6)	194	M.M. ♩. =	84	(14)	456	M.M. ♩. =	80
(7)	225	M.M. ♩ =	100	(15)	522	M.M. ♩ =	112
(8)	248	M.M. ♩ =	92	(16)	526	M.M. ♩ =	80

(*Return* to page *113*)

EXERCISE 11.9

Anacrusis

In the last measure of each example, place one note which will make a complete measure when added to the anacrusis.

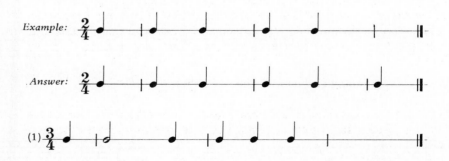

(*Return* to page *113*)

EXERCISE 11.10

Writing rhythmic syllables

Below each note write the rhythmic syllable.

EXERCISE 11.11

Rhythmic reading (with the syllables written out)

While conducting and tapping the meter, read aloud the rhythmic syllables for each of the examples in Exercise 11.10.

EXERCISE 11.12

Rhythmic reading, simple meter

While conducting and tapping the meter, read with rhythmic syllables the rhythm of the melodies found in Exercise 7.2T. For additional practice, read the rhythm patterns and the rhythm of melodies from *Music for Sight Singing*, Chapters 1 and 2.

EXERCISE 11.13

Rhythmic reading, compound meter

While conducting and tapping the meter, read the rhythm of the melodies found in Exercise 7.4T. For additional practice, read the rhythm patterns and the rhythm of melodies from *Music for Sight Singing*, Chapter 3.

EXERCISE 11.14

Rhythmic reading, simple and compound meters

While conducting and tapping the meter, read the rhythm of the melodies found in Exercise 7.5T. For additional practice, read melodies from *Music for Sight Singing*, Chapter 4, Sections 1 and 2, and Chapter 5, Sections 1–5.

CHAPTER TWELVE

Time
(continued)

Beams in Notation
Rests in Notation
Rhythmic Transcription
Rhythmic Dictation

The next skill to be developed after rhythmic reading is the ability to identify the rhythm of a melodic line when you hear it and to write it on paper as notation. This process of writing the rhythmic pattern you hear is called *rhythmic dictation*. Just as a stenographer in the world of business "takes dictation," so in music the student also "takes dictation." Rhythmic dictation is, in a sense, the reverse process of rhythmic reading. In rhythmic reading notation is transferred into sound; in rhythmic dictation sound is transferred into notation. In order to write correctly the rhythm you hear, you must understand certain principles of the use of *beams* and *rests in notation*.

Beams in Notation

Beams have been previously described as heavy lines that connect the stems of notes. Beams make notation easier to read by (1) eliminating long series of flagged notes and (2) clarifying the location of the beats in a measure. Figure 12.1 shows a measure of 9/8 meter containing nine eighth notes written in three different ways. In Figure 12.1*a* the notation is correct, but in Figure 12.1*b* the notation is easier to read because the beams clarify the location of each of the three beats in triple compound meter. Incorrect beaming, as seen in Figure 12.1*c*, actually makes the same rhythmic pattern more difficult to read

FIGURE 12.1   *Use of Beams.*

because the beginnings of beamed groups do not coincide with the second and third beats of triple compound meter.

A beam once begun does not ordinarily extend into the next beat unit.[1] If additional notes are to be beamed, a new beam will start at the new beat, as shown in Figure 12.2. The following examples show various correct and incorrect applications of this principle. The bracket (⌐____⌐) indicates the duration of a beat.

FIGURE 12.2 *Correct and Incorrect Uses of Beams.*

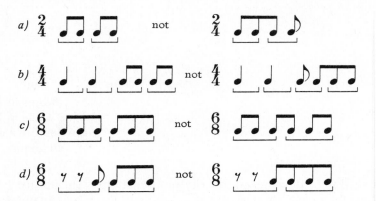

EXERCISES
12.1, 12.2

Rests in Notation

1. *Dotted Rests.* Rests, like notes, may be dotted. The dot increases the value of the rest by one-half, e.g., 𝄾· = 𝄾 𝄿, 𝄾· = 𝄿 𝄾, ▬· = ▬𝄿; etc.

2. *The Whole Rest.* Whenever an entire measure is to be silent, a whole rest is written, whatever the meter signature in use at the time.

FIGURE 12.3 *Use of the Whole Rest.*

a) $\frac{3}{4}$ 𝅗𝅥. | ▬ | 𝅗𝅥.   ‖

b) $\frac{6}{8}$ 𝅗𝅥.   𝅗𝅥. | ▬ | 𝅗𝅥.   ‖

3. *Separate or Combined Rests.*
    a. When a period of silence lasts more than one beat, individual (separate) rests may be used for each beat, or, when the silence begins on a strong beat, rests may be combined and shown as a single rest. For example,

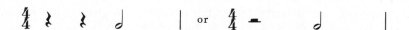

1. Exceptions will be found in actual music, but always with good cause. You should adhere to the basic principles for writing beams and rests presented in this chapter until, in later study, you become experienced in the intricacies of music editing.

b. If a combining of rests would make the location of the beats of a measure unclear, separate rests should be used. In Figure 12.4 each example in the right-hand column contains a rest which obscures the location of one of the beats of the measure.

FIGURE 12.4 *Correct and Incorrect Uses of Rests.*

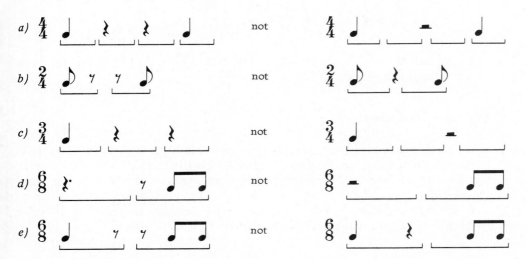

c. In compound meter, separate rests are ordinarily used for the second and third divisions of the beat; for example,

EXERCISE 12.3

While composers write much music in the familiar $\frac{2}{4}$, $\frac{3}{4}$, $\frac{4}{4}$, and $\frac{6}{8}$ time signatures, they frequently employ a variety of other signatures. You can develop the ability to work confidently in a wide range of time signatures through exercises in *rhythmic transcription*.

Rhythmic Transcription

Rhythmic transcription is the rewriting of a piece using a meter signature with the same numerator but a different denominator. This will produce a notation that looks different from the original but sounds identical when performed. For example, when you hear a rhythmic pattern in quadruple simple time there is no way of knowing what the notation will be until you are told, or decide for yourself, the bottom number of the meter signature. A pattern in quadruple simple meter can be written using a half note, a quarter note, or an eighth note as the beat unit. Although the notation looks different, each one will actually sound exactly like the others, assuming all have the same tempo indication. In Figure 12.5, the solutions are identical in sound (when the tempo for the beat unit is the same); only the notation is different.

FIGURE 12.5 *Rhythmic Transcription.*

EXERCISE
12.4

We have now reinforced some of the important concepts of notation and are ready to begin the study of *rhythmic dictation.*

Rhythmic Dictation

We are now ready to listen to a melody and to write the rhythm of this melody, using notation, on paper. To develop most efficiently the skill of taking rhythmic dictation, follow these systematic steps in *listening to a melody* and *writing the rhythm.*

Listening to a Melody. When the instructor is ready to play a melody for rhythmic dictation, observe this procedure:

Step 1. The meter signature will be announced. Using the appropriate conductor's beat and tapping the divisions, follow the instructor's lead in establishing the meter. Students continue to conduct and tap throughout Steps 2, 3, and 4.

Step 2. As the instructor plays, listen to the melody and commit it to memory.

Step 3. Sing back the melody, using the neutral syllable *la.*

Step 4. Sing the melody again, this time using rhythmic syllables, *or* recite without pitch using rhythmic syllables. For Figure 12.7 these syllables would be "one two three-ta four-ta / one two three."

Writing the Rhythm. For the first exercises in rhythmic dictation, diagrams are supplied to help you in writing the notation. Each diagram consists of three lines:

1. *The top line* shows the beat durations of each measure (the same as the right-hand conductor's beat)

2. *The bottom line* shows the beat divisions of each measure (the same as the left-hand division)

3. On *the middle line* you are to write the rhythm.

FIGURE 12.6 *Rhythmic Dictation: Meter Diagram.*

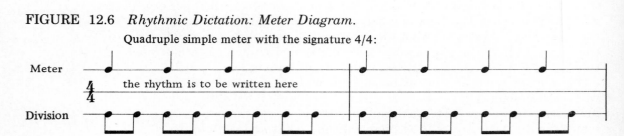

Figure 12.7a shows a rhythmic dictation problem as played by the instructor. The solution, b), is the rhythmic pattern placed on the middle line of the diagram.

FIGURE 12.7 *Example of Rhythmic Dictation.*

a) Problem played by the instructor:

b) Solution written on the middle line:

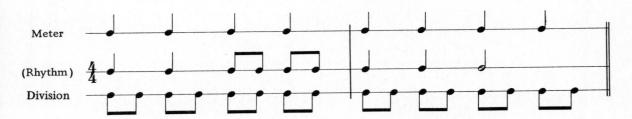

Meter

(Rhythm)

Division

EXERCISES
12.5T, 12.6T

EXERCISE 12.1

Improving notation by use of beams

Rewrite each rhythmic pattern by using beams where feasible.

EXERCISE 12.2

Correcting examples showing incorrect use of beams

Rewrite each exercise with correct beaming.

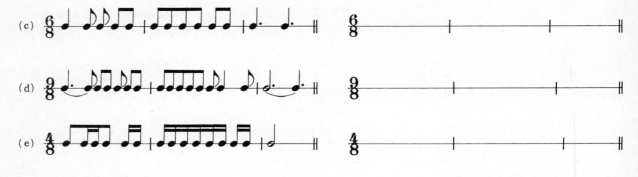

(*Return* to page *122*)

EXERCISE 12.3

Correcting examples showing incorrect use of rests

Rewrite each exercise with correct rests.

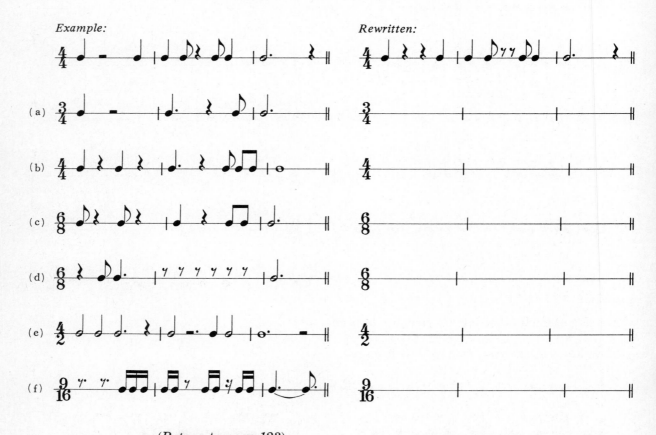

(*Return* to page *123*)

EXERCISE 12.4

Rhythmic transcription

Rewrite each given rhythm (*a*) using the meter signatures indicated in (*b*) and (*c*).

NAME ______________________________

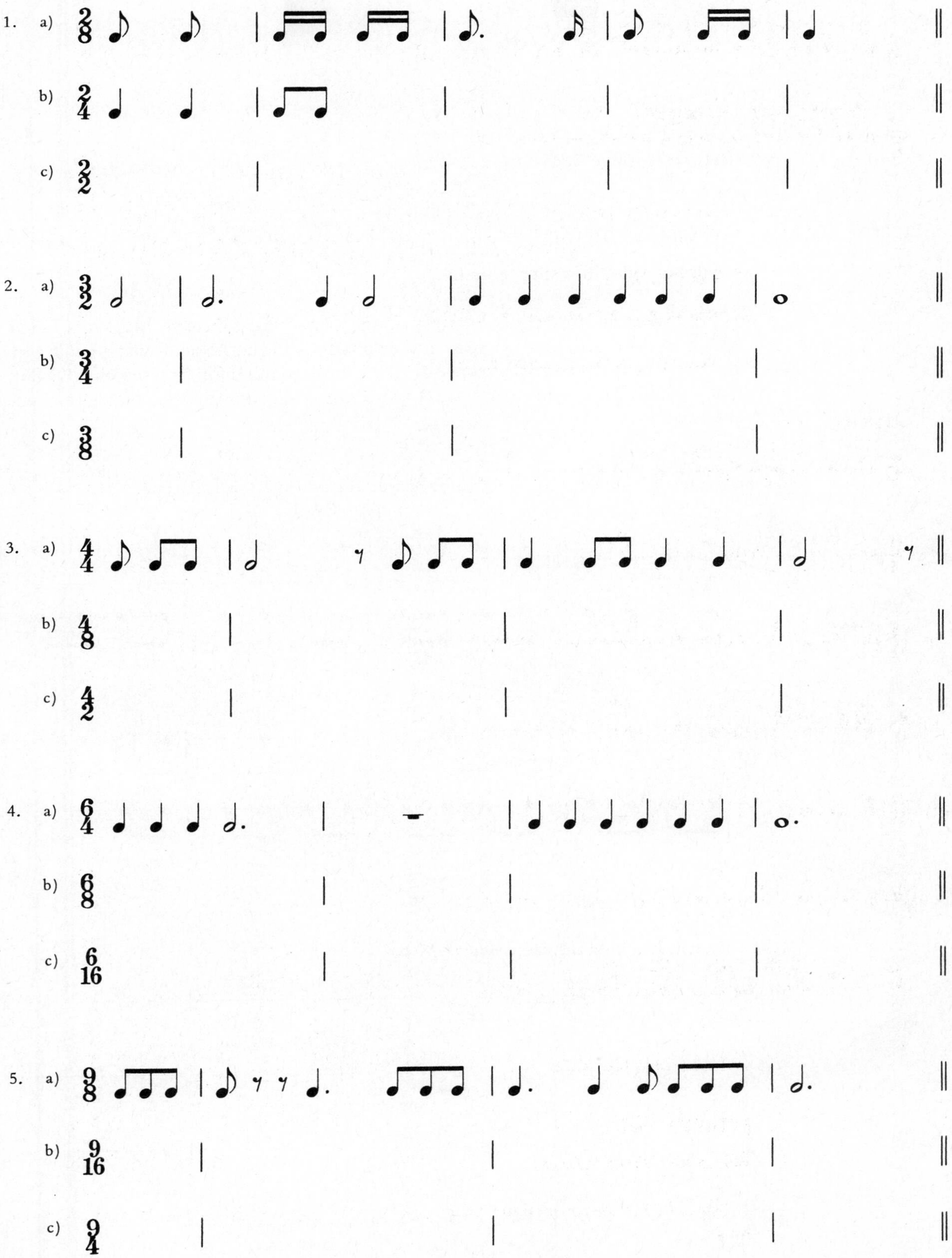

1. a) 2/8
b) 2/4
c) 2/2
2. a) 3/2
b) 3/4
c) 3/8
3. a) 4/4
b) 4/8
c) 4/2
4. a) 6/4
b) 6/8
c) 6/16
5. a) 9/8
b) 9/16
c) 9/4

6. a) b) c)

(*Return* to page *124*)

EXERCISE 12.5T

Rhythmic dictation, simple meter

Follow basic directions given on pages 124–25. Observe headings below which list contents of exercises and/or changes in methods of writing. The instructor will play from correspondingly numbered melodies on pages 133-35. Upon completion of an exercise, the student may turn to these pages to check the answer.

Group A. Duple simple meter; ♩ = 1 beat; begin on the downbeat; use diagram.

Write answers when only the center line is given.

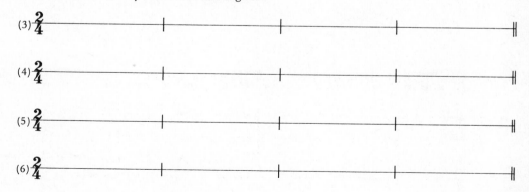

Group B. Triple simple meter; ♩ = 1 beat; begin on the downbeat; use diagram.

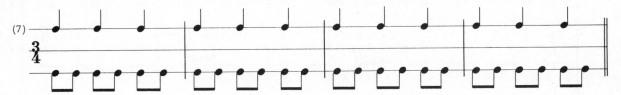

Write answers when only the center line is given.

Group C. Quadruple simple meter; ♩ = 1 beat begin on the downbeat; use diagram.

Write answers when only the center line is given.

Group D. Simple meter; ♩ = 1 beat; begin on the upbeat; use diagram.

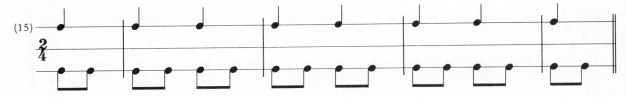

(16)

(17)

Write answers when only the center line is given.

(18)

(19)

(20)

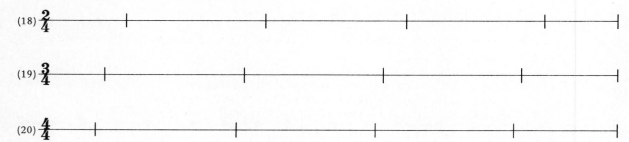

Group E. Simple time; ♩ or ♪ = 1 beat; use diagram.

(21)

(22)

(23)

Write answers when only the center line is given.

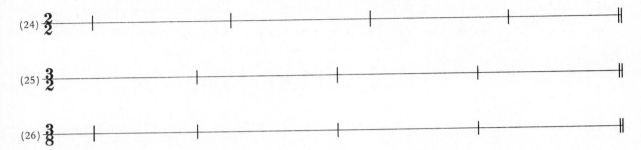

(24)

(25)

(26)

Group F. Melodies 27-36. Various simple meter signatures. Write your answers without benefit of lines, using any convenient piece of paper.

(*Instructor:* For additional material for dictation in simple meters, use melodies or excerpts of melodies from *Music for Sight Singing,* Chapters 1 and 2, or from *More Music for Sight Singing,* melodies 266–307.)

Dictation material for Exercise 12.5T

The symbol ' found in each of these exercises indicates a convenient place to divide the exercise into two sections, should the entire exercise prove to be overly long.

Group A

(1) (2)

(3) (4)

(5) (6)

Group B

(7) (8)

Group C

Group D

Group E

Group F

EXERCISE 12.6T

Rhythmic dictation, compound meter

Follow basic directions given on pages 124-25. Observe headings below which list contents of exercises and/or changes in methods of writing. The instructor will play from correspondingly numbered melodies on pages 138-39. Upon completion of an exercise, the student may turn to these pages to check the answer.

The instructor may divide any example into two two-measure sections if shorter exercises are desired.

Group A. Duple compound meter; ♩.=1 beat; begin on the downbeat; use diagram.

Write answers when only the center line is given.

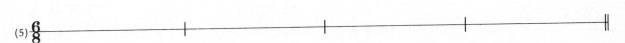

Group B. Triple compound meter; ♩.=1 beat; begin on the downbeat; use diagram.

(6)

Write answer when only the center line is given.

(7)

Group C. Quadruple compound meter; ♩.=1 beat; begin on the downbeat; use diagram.

(8)

Write answer when only the center line is given.

(9)

Group D. Compound meter; ♩.=1 beat; begin on the upbeat; use diagram. In compound meter, the upbeat may be a ♩. or a smaller note value. In the last measure, be sure that the note values consider the anacrusis.

(10)

(11)

136

(12)

Write answer when only the center line is given.

(13) 6/8

(14) 9/8

(15) 12/8

Group E. Compound meter ♩. or ♪.=1 beat; use diagram.

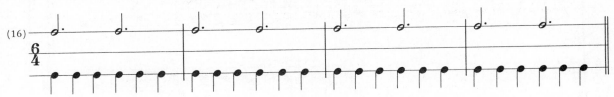

(16) 6/4

(17) The upbeat occures on a beat division. The notation in the final measure will consequently be less than a full measure though a full measure of diagram is supplied.

6/16

Group F. Melodies 18-24. Various compound meter signatures. Write your answer without benefit of diagrams or lines using any convenient piece of paper.

(*Instructor:* For additional material for dictation in compound meters, use melodies or excerpts of melodies from *Music for Sight Singing*, Chapter 3, and Section 2 of Chapter 4, or, from *More Music for Sight Singing*, melodies 308–331 as well as those melodies in compound time between 332 and 384.)

Dictation material for Exercise 12.6T

Group E

(16)

(17)

Group F

(18)

(19)

(20)

(21)

(22)

(23)

(24)

139

CHAPTER THIRTEEN

Pitch:
Minor Scales

Accidentals, continued
Minor Scales: Natural (Pure), Harmonic and Melodic Forms
Use of Minor Scales

It was observed in Chapter 10 that much of the music commonly performed today is based on two different scales, major and minor. We have learned that the sound of a scale is determined by the location of half steps and whole steps in the scale. Therefore, we can expect that the minor scale, which sounds different from the major scale, will have a different arrangement of half steps and whole steps. This is true, but there are actually three different forms of the minor scale.

Writing certain minor scales requires use of accidentals in addition to sharps and flats. Therefore, we will first study the remaining accidentals: the *double sharp, double flat,*[1] and *natural sign* (listed on page 19).

Accidentals, Continued:
Double Sharp, Double Flat, and Natural Sign

The *double sharp,* ×, raises the pitch of a note two half steps or one whole step.

FIGURE 13.1 *The Double Sharp.*

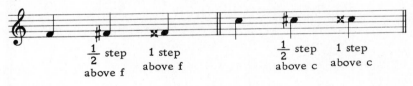

$\frac{1}{2}$ step above f   1 step above f $\frac{1}{2}$ step above c   1 step above c

It can be seen that a note carrying a double sharp will always be enharmonic with another pitch name. In Figure 13.1, F× is enharmonic with the pitch G; C× is enharmonic with D.

The *double flat,* ♭♭, lowers the pitch of a note two half steps or one whole step.

---

1. Though not found in major or minor scale spelling, the double flat is included here to complete the study of accidentals.

141

FIGURE 13.2 *The Double Flat.*

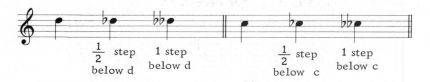

$\frac{1}{2}$ step below d 1 step below d $\frac{1}{2}$ step below c 1 step below c

D♭♭ is enharmonic with C; C♭♭ is enharmonic with B♭.

The *natural sign,* ♮, cancels a previously used accidental, or the accidental in the key signature.

FIGURE 13.3 *The Natural Sign.*

d   d♯   d   c♯   c   b♭   d♭   d   b♭   b

Considerations in Using Accidentals. (*a*) Any accidental placed before a note affects the pitch on that line or space only.

d   c   c♯   d

(*b*) The effect of an accidental lasts only until the next bar line.

d   c   b   c   d   c♯   b   c♯   d

(*c*) An accidental may be used optionally as a reminder. The preceding illustration is repeated below with the reminder in measure two. The ♯ before C does not imply double sharp.

d   c   b   c   d   c♯   b   c♯   d

(*d*) When it is necessary for a note to carry a double sharp or a double flat, the symbol ✕ or ♭♭ is always used, even if there is already a sharp or flat in the signature.

f♯   f✕   e♭   e♭♭

(*e*) When it is necessary to place a sharp or double sharp before a note already carrying a flat, or to place a flat or double flat before a note already car-

142

rying a sharp, the natural sign has traditionally preceded the new accidental, but in current practice is no longer necessary.

Now that we are informed in the use of accidentals, we are ready to proceed to the study of the minor scale and its three forms, *natural (pure)*, *harmonic,* and *melodic.*

The Natural (Pure) Form of the Minor Scale

The *natural (pure)* form of the minor scale consists of a series of eight tones with the following succession of intervals between tones: whole step, half step, whole step, whole step, half step, whole step, whole step.

FIGURE 13.4   *Structure of the Natural (Pure) Minor Scale.*

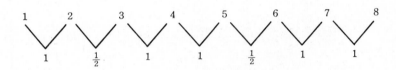

It can be seen that the natural minor scale consists of whole steps except between the second and third degrees and the fifth and sixth degrees, where the intervals are half steps. On a keyboard, notice that the natural minor scale starting on A involves only white keys because the half steps 2-3 and 5-6 coincide with the white keys B-C and E-F.

FIGURE 13.5   *The A Minor Scale, Natural Form.*

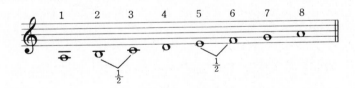

All natural minor scales starting on pitches other than A require one or more accidentals in order to maintain the characteristic half step and whole step pattern of the scale structure shown in Figure 13.4. For example, the natural minor scale of E requires one sharp.

FIGURE 13.6   *The E Minor Scale, Natural Form.*

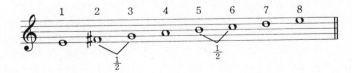

143

As with major scales, there are seven natural minor scales containing sharps and seven containing flats, which, including A minor (no sharps or flats) comprise the fifteen natural minor scales.

FIGURE 13.7 *Table of Minor Scales and Numbers of Accidentals for the Natural Form.*

Scale	A	E	B	F♯	C♯	G♯	D♯	A♯
Accidentals	none	1♯	2♯	3♯	4♯	5♯	6♯	7♯
Scale		D	G	C	F	B♭	E♭	A♭
Accidentals		1♭	2♭	3♭	4♭	5♭	6♭	7♭

Figure 13.7 also shows relationship by fifths between minor scales, as we saw earlier in major scales. The circle of fifths for minor scales will be studied in Chapter 16.

Harmonic Form of the Minor Scale

The *harmonic form* of the minor scale is derived from the natural form: it is the natural form but with a raised seventh degree.

FIGURE 13.8 *The A Minor Scale, Harmonic Form.*

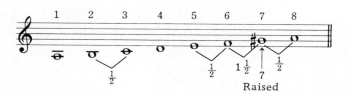

Notice that by raising the seventh, the interval between 6 and 7 becomes a step-and-a-half (three half steps), and the interval between 7 and 8 becomes a half step. Any natural minor scale can be changed to the harmonic form by raising the seventh scale degree. For example, the E natural minor scale shown in Figure 13.6 becomes the harmonic form when the seventh, D, is raised by the sharp.

FIGURE 13.9 *The E Minor Scale, Harmonic Form.*

Melodic Form of the Minor Scale

The *melodic form* of the minor scale is derived from the natural form. Unlike all other major and minor scales, its ascending and descending forms are different. The ascending form of the melodic minor scale is the natural form but with *raised sixth and raised seventh degrees*. The descending form is the same as the natural form; the *seventh and sixth degrees are lowered* from their ascending form. The descending seventh and sixth scale degrees are often called "lowered" even though they are natural scale steps. Actually, they are lowered only in relation to the ascending form of the melodic minor scale.

FIGURE 13.10 *The A Minor Scale, Melodic Form.*

Any natural minor scale can be changed to the melodic form by (1) raising the sixth and seventh degrees in the ascending scale structure and (2) lowering the sixth and seventh scale degrees to their natural form in the descending scale structure. For example, the E natural minor scale shown in Figure 13.6 becomes the ascending melodic form shown in Figure 13.11 when the sixth scale degree C and the seventh degree D are raised by sharps. In descending, the seventh and sixth are lowered by natural signs; the descending scale is identical to the natural form.

FIGURE 13.11 *The E Minor Scale, Melodic Form.*

Figure 13.12 shows a comparison of the three different forms of the minor scale.

FIGURE 13.12 *A Minor: Natural, Harmonic and Melodic Forms.*

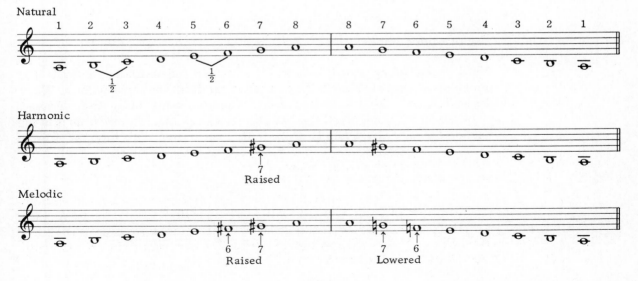

Several minor scales require use of the double sharp, as in the G♯ minor scale, harmonic form:

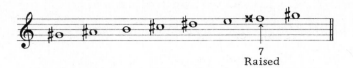

The natural sign is sometimes required to raise a pitch, as in the B♭ minor scale:

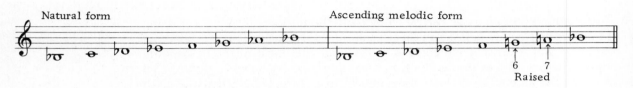

EXERCISE
13.1

As we discovered previously in working with major scales, it is useful to be able to spell (write) scales by letter names using appropriate accidentals. Remember that the name of the accidental comes after the letter. As a rule, the natural sign is optional in spelling.

FIGURE 13.13 *Spelling the B Minor Scale, Three Forms.*

Natural:	B	C♯	D	E	F♯	G	A	B
Harmonic:	B	C♯	D	E	F♯	G	A♯	B
Melodic,								
ascending:	B	C♯	D	E	F♯	G♯	A♯	B
descending:	B	A(♮)	G(♮)	F♯	E	D	C♯	B

EXERCISE
13.2

Use of Minor Scales

When an ascending melody displays raised sixth and seventh scale steps in a minor scale, it is obvious that these notes are from the melodic form. When descending, the melody usually displays lowered seventh and sixth scale steps.

In measure 3 of Figure 13.14, had the F♯ been F♮, the distance from it to the leading tone (F♮-G♯) would be more than a whole step. This interval of three

FIGURE 13.14 *Use of the Melodic Form of the Minor Scale.*

Bach, *Herr, straf mich nicht in deinem Zorn*

146

half steps (a step-and-a-half[2]) has been found objectionable by most composers and performers, except in certain circumstances. Raising the sixth scale step eliminates this awkward interval while still retaining a leading tone.

Confusion about scale formation, whether melodic or harmonic, often exists when the lowered sixth scale step and the raised seventh (or vice versa) are separated by intervening tones; this is the way in which these two tones are most frequently found.

FIGURE 13.15 *Characteristic Tones in the Minor Scale.*

Schubert, *Erstarrung*

Use of F♮ and G♯ from the A minor scale would seem to indicate the harmonic form of the scale. Yet each of these tones is used as being in the melodic form of the scale: the seventh scale step, G♯, is raised because it ascends; the sixth scale step, F♮, is lowered because it descends.

The melodic minor, as its name implies, is especially suited for melody writing because it explains situations involving the sixth and seventh scale steps. Therefore, most melodies in minor can be described as exhibiting characteristics of the melodic minor scale, unless obvious characteristics of the other forms are displayed.[3]

Melodies which display adjacent lowered sixth and raised seventh scale steps as in the harmonic minor scale are not rare, but are less commonly found.

The interval of a step-and-a-half between 6 and 7 of the harmonic minor scale (in Figure 13.16 shown descending ♯7-♭6) is somewhat awkward to perform, both in instrumental and, particularly, in vocal music. This accounts for the sparing use of the harmonic minor scale in melodic writing.

FIGURE 13.16 *Use of Harmonic Form of the Minor Scale.*

Beethoven, Quartet Op. 59, No. 3

D minor, harmonic: D E F G A B♭ C♯ D

Melodies using the natural form of the scale are actually making use of one of the *medieval modes* (the Aeolian) from a system of six early scale forms.[4] These were in general use up to the seventeenth century in composed music; they are frequently found in folk music of the Western world both from that

2. Called *augmented second;* included in the study of intervals, Chapter 18.
3. Intervallic leaps from the sixth and seventh scale steps may also be found in melodic writing. Explanation of these and other melodic considerations must be deferred until study of theory more advanced than is presented in this text.
4. The medieval modes are described in Appendix 3. Many examples of all modes in both composed and folk music can be found in *Music for Sight Singing*, Chapter 15. See also *More Music for Sight Singing*, Part IV.

era and from later centuries; and in the present century they have found favor in all styles of composition, including jazz and popular music. The folk song in Figure 13.17 uses the Aeolian mode, or natural form of the minor scale.

FIGURE 13.17 *Use of Natural Form of the Minor Scale.*

England

D minor, natural: D E F G A B♭ C D

EXERCISE
13.3

EXERCISE 13.2

Spelling minor scales

Write minor scales using letter names with accidentals where needed. Indicate half steps in the natural minor and the additional accidentals needed in the harmonic and melodic forms.

Example: C minor (spell the three forms of the C minor scale)

Answer: Natural

Harmonic

Melodic

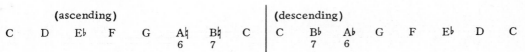

(1) A minor
Natural

Harmonic

Melodic

(2) E minor
Natural

Harmonic

Melodic

157

(3) D minor
Natural

Harmonic

Melodic

(4) G minor
Natural

Harmonic

Melodic

(5) F♯ minor
Natural

Harmonic

Melodic

(6) F minor
Natural

Harmonic

Melodic

(7) C♯ minor

Natural

Harmonic

Melodic

For additional practice, spell the three forms of these scales: B♭ minor, G♯ minor, E♭ minor, D♯ minor, A♭ minor, and A♯ minor.

(*Return* to page *146*)

EXERCISE 13.3

Identifying the forms of the minor scale

Each of the following melodies uses a particular form of the minor scale. The first scale tone (tonic) is given and shown on the staff (●). In the blank space, identify the scale as natural, harmonic, or melodic.

Example: Beethoven, Quartet, Op. 59, No. 3

A minor, _____ harmonic _____ form

(1)   Brahms, *Ballade*, Op. 118, No. 3

G minor, _____ MELODIC _____ form

(2)   England

D minor, _____ NATURAL _____ form

(3)   Bach, Lute Suite, BWV 996

E minor, _____MELODIC_____ form

(4)   God Rest Ye Merry, Gentlemen

C minor, _____ form

(5)   Paganini, *Caprice*, Op. 1, No. 6

G minor, _____ form

CHAPTER FOURTEEN

Pitch: Minor Scales (continued)

Names of Scale Degrees in Minor
Playing Minor Scales at the Keyboard
Singing Minor Scales

Scale degrees in minor use the same names as scale degrees in major (Chapter 6), but because of the alteration of the 6th and 7th steps, additional terminology is required for *names of scale degrees in minor*.

Names of Scale Degrees in Minor

The term *leading tone* in minor refers to the tone one half step below the tonic, just as in major. Therefore, in minor, the leading tone is the raised seventh scale degree. When the seventh degree is not raised it is known as the *subtonic*.

FIGURE 14.1 *The Leading Tone and Subtonic in the Minor Scale.*

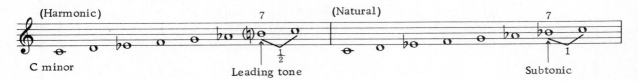

Submediant in minor refers to the natural sixth scale step. When the sixth scale step is raised it is called *raised submediant*.

FIGURE 14.2 *The Submediant and Raised Submediant in the Minor Scale.*

161

The ascending and descending melodic minor scale displays all possible scale degree names.

FIGURE 14.3 *Names of the Scale Degrees in Melodic Minor.*

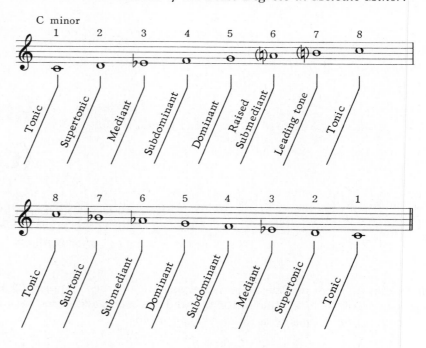

EXERCISES
14.1, 14.2

The minor scales are played following the same procedures outlined in Chapter 8 for playing major scales.

Playing Minor Scales at the Keyboard[1]

The A Minor Scale

By playing the white key A and the next seven white keys above it, an A minor scale (natural form) will be produced. Playing only white keys from this given pitch A automatically places the half steps in their correct scale locations, between 2 and 3 and between 5 and 6, as shown in Figure 14.4.

FIGURE 14.4 *Playing the A Minor Scale, Natural Form.*

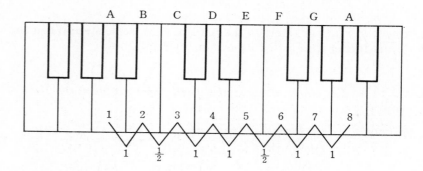

1. See Appendix 4, page 287, for fingering of minor scales.

162

To play the harmonic form of the A minor scale, raise the seventh scale step G to G♯.

FIGURE 14.5   *Playing the A Minor Scale, Harmonic Form.*

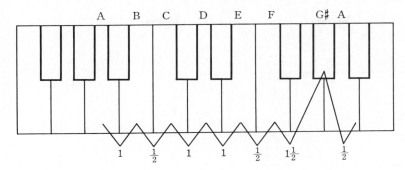

To play the melodic form of the A minor scale, raise the sixth scale step F to F♯ and the seventh scale step G to G♯ when ascending.

FIGURE 14.6   *Playing the A Minor Scale, Melodic Form.*

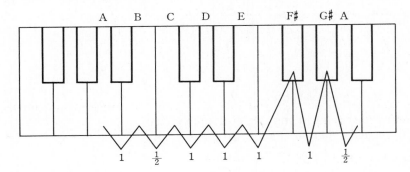

When descending, play the natural form of the scale as shown in Figure 14.4.

All Other Minor Scales Except Those on G♯, D♯, and A♯

To play any minor scale, keep in mind the familiar pattern for the natural form with half steps between 2-3 and 5-6. Determine the succession of keys on the keyboard needed to produce the natural form, then alter as necessary for the harmonic and melodic forms. Figure 14.7 shows the keys needed to play the three forms of the B♭ minor scale.

FIGURE 14.7   *Playing the B♭ Minor Scale.*

Natural form

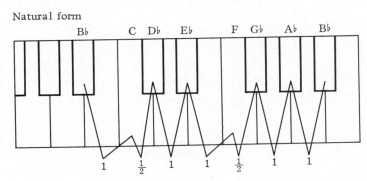

163

Harmonic form

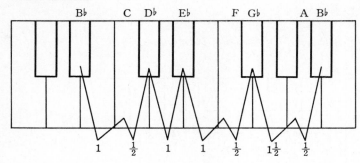

Melodic form

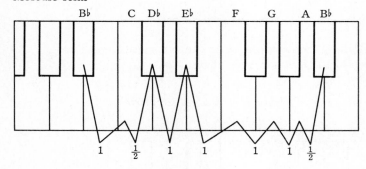

To play this scale descending, use the natural form

Minor Scales on G♯, D♯, and A♯

These scales require the use of double sharps.
These specific double sharps are used:

G♯ minor	raised 7th scale step	F✕
D♯ minor	raised 7th scale step	C✕
A♯ minor	raised 6th scale step	F✕
	raised 7th scale step	G✕

Here is how these doubly sharped notes appear on the keyboard:

FIGURE 14.8 *Locating C✕, F✕ and G✕ on the Keyboard.*

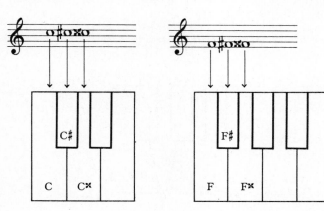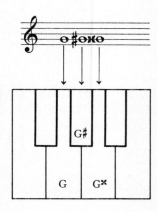

In the G♯ minor scale shown below the ✕ is used to raise the seventh scale degree (F♯) one half step up to F✕.

FIGURE 14.9 *Playing the G♯ Minor Scale.*

Natural form

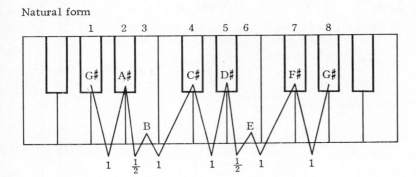

Harmonic form

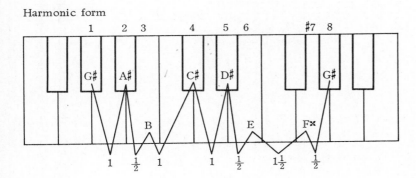

Melodic form

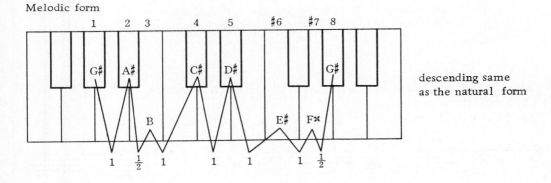

descending same as the natural form

In addition to the foregoing procedures, you will also find that your previous experience in playing major scales will be helpful in playing minor scales due to the similarities between a given major scale and the minor scale using the same tonic note.[2]

2. Most, but not all, major and minor scales share a common tonic. Exceptions are major scales D♭, G♭, C♭, and minor scales G♯, D♯, and A♯.

Major scale →	lower its third scale step	=	minor scale, melodic form ascending
Major scale →	lower its third and sixth scale steps	=	minor scale, harmonic form
Major scale →	lower its third, sixth, and seventh scale steps	=	minor scale, natural form

FIGURE 14.10 *Comparing Major and Minor Scales.*

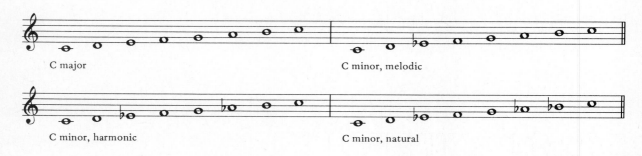

C major

C minor, melodic

C minor, harmonic

C minor, natural

**EXERCISES
14.3, 14.4,
14.5**

Singing Minor Scales

Minor scales can be sung using the three methods practiced in singing major scales: by numbers, by letter names, and by syllables. In public schools, the syllable most widely used for singing the tonic in a minor scale is *la*.[3] Figure 14.11 shows application of the three methods for singing all forms of minor scales.

FIGURE 14.11 *Singing the Three Forms of the Minor Scale on Numbers, Letter Names and Syllables, in C Minor.*

Natural

Sing																
Numbers :	1	2	3	4	5	6	7	8	8	7	6	5	4	3	2	1
Letters :	c	d	eb	f	g	ab	bb	c	c	bb	ab	g	f	eb	d	c
Syllables :	la	ti	do	re	mi	fa	sol	la	la	sol	fa	mi	re	do	ti	la

3. The relationship of syllables in major and minor will be shown in Chapter 16.

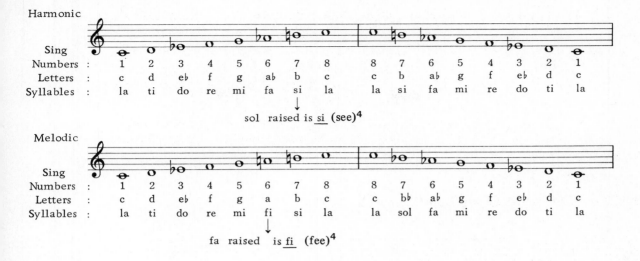

Harmonic

Sing																
Numbers :	1	2	3	4	5	6	7	8	8	7	6	5	4	3	2	1
Letters :	c	d	e♭	f	g	a♭	b	c	c	b	a♭	g	f	e♭	d	c
Syllables :	la	ti	do	re	mi	fa	si	la	la	si	fa	mi	re	do	ti	la

sol raised is <u>si</u> (see)[4]

Melodic

Sing																
Numbers :	1	2	3	4	5	6	7	8	8	7	6	5	4	3	2	1
Letters :	c	d	e♭	f	g	a	b	c	c	b♭	a♭	g	f	e♭	d	c
Syllables :	la	ti	do	re	mi	fi	si	la	la	sol	fa	mi	re	do	ti	la

fa raised is <u>fi</u> (fee)[4]

EXERCISE
14.6

4. For chromatic syllables, see Appendix 3.

EXERCISE 14.1

Naming scale degrees in minor

Supply names of the scale degrees for the different scales given below:

(1) E minor, natural form

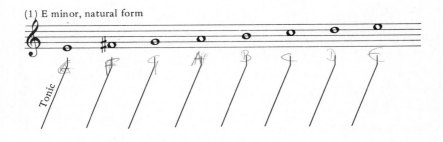

Tonic E F♯ G A♭ B C D E

(2) E minor, harmonic form

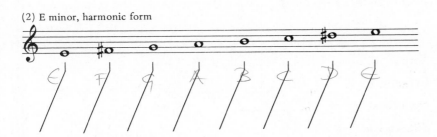

E F G A B C D E

(3) E minor, melodic form

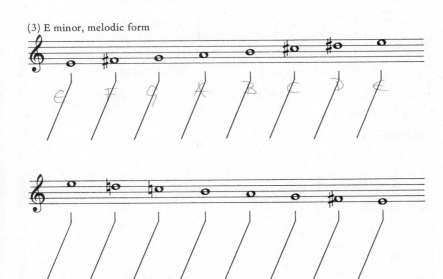

E F G A B C D E

(4) F# minor, melodic form (only)

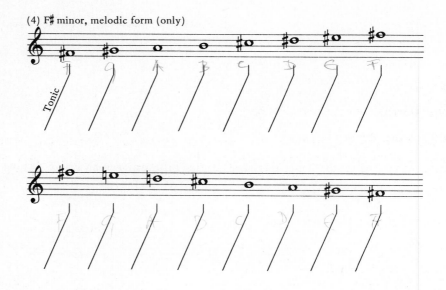

Tonic

EXERCISE 14.2

Identifying scale degrees in minor

Give the pitch name for each scale degree listed; the tonic is identified.

(1) Tonic — A
     Leading tone — G#
     Dominant — E
     Supertonic — _____
     Subtonic — _____
     Submediant — _____
     Subdominant — _____
     Mediant — _____
     Raised submediant — _____

(2) Tonic — D
     Subdominant — G
     Subtonic — C
     Mediant — F
     Raised submediant — ♮B
     Submediant — ♭b
     Supertonic — _____
     Dominant — A
     Leading tone — C#

(3) Tonic — B
     Mediant — D
     Subtonic — ♮A
     Submediant — ♮G
     Leading tone — #A
     Supertonic — C#
     Raised submediant — G#
     Dominant — F#
     Subdominant — E

(4) Tonic — G
     Submediant — E♭
     Supertonic — A
     Subtonic — F
     Leading tone — F#
     Subdominant — C
     Mediant — B♭
     Raised submediant — E♮
     Dominant — D

(*Return* to page *162*)

NAME _____

EXERCISE 14.3

Playing minor scales at the keyboard

Using the example as a guide, (1) indicate by arrows and by numbers 1-8 the keys on the keyboard required to produce the sound of the scale, (2) indicate whole steps and half steps, and (3), play the scale (for the melodic form, play ascending and descending).

Example: B♭ Minor.

Natural form

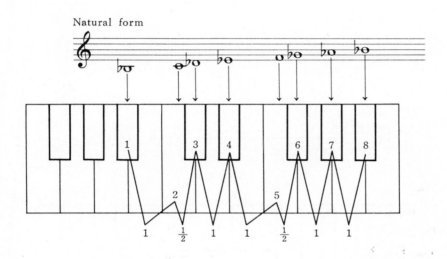

Harmonic form

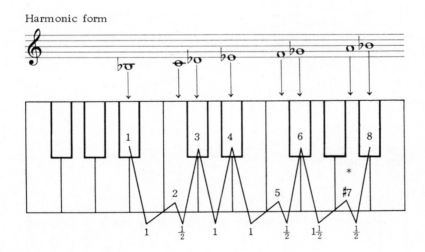

*In this context, " ♯ " simply means "raised," referring to a change from the natural form of the minor scale.

Melodic form (When descending, use natural form)

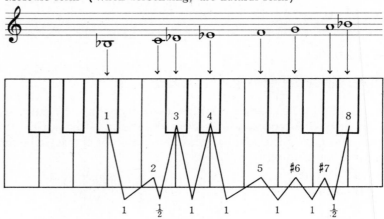

(1) G Minor
natural form

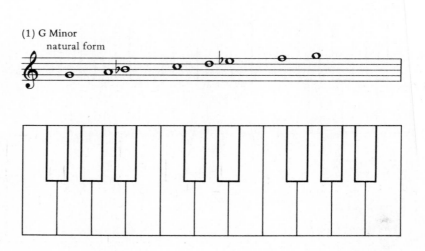

harmonic form

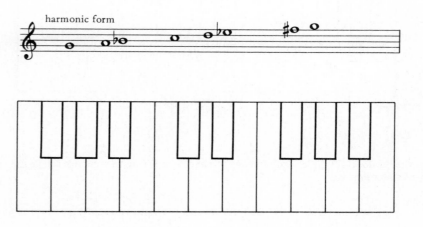

172

melodic form, ascending

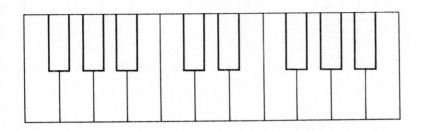

(2) F Minor, natural form (only)

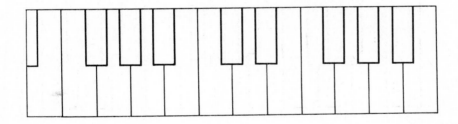

(3) C#Minor, harmonic form

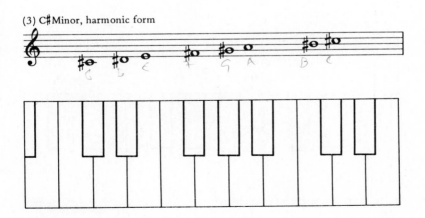

(4) D♯ Minor, melodic form, ascending

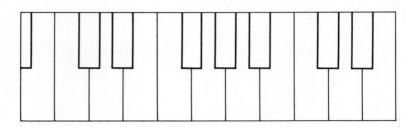

EXERCISE 14.4

Playing minor scales at the keyboard

This exercise is similar to Exercise 14.3, but without the staff. Number the keys, indicate whole steps and half steps, and then play.

(1) E Minor, natural form

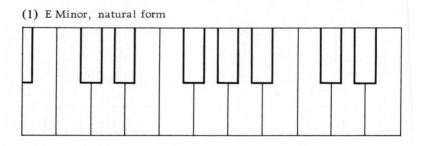

(2) D Minor, harmonic form

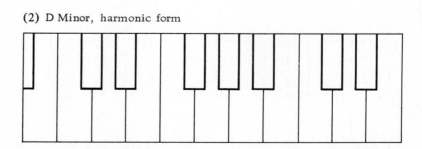

CHAPTER FIFTEEN

Pitch:
Minor Key
Signatures

Circle of Fifths for Minor Keys
Minor Key Signatures on the Staff

The function of the key signature is the same in minor as it is in major (Chapter 10). The key signature in minor uses the accidentals found in the natural (pure) form of the scale. If the accidentals in the scale are extracted and grouped together they will form the particular minor key signature. Including A minor (no sharps or flats), there are fifteen minor key signatures.

FIGURE 15.1 *Number and Names of Accidentals for Minor Key Signatures.*

Name of minor key	Number of #'s or ♭'s in key signature	Names of #'s or ♭'s						
A minor	none							
E minor	1♯	f♯						
B minor	2♯	f♯,	c♯					
F♯ minor	3♯	f♯,	c♯,	g♯				
C♯ minor	4♯	f♯,	c♯,	g♯,	d♯			
G♯ minor	5♯	f♯,	c♯,	g♯,	d♯,	a♯		
D♯ minor	6♯	f♯,	c♯,	g♯,	d♯,	a♯,	e♯	
A♯ minor	7♯	f♯,	c♯,	g♯,	d♯,	a♯,	e♯,	b♯
(A minor)	(none)							
D minor	1♭	b♭						
G minor	2♭	b♭	e♭					

Name of minor key	Number of ♯'s or ♭'s in key signature	Names of ♯'s or ♭'s						
C minor	3♭	b♭	e♭	a♭				
F minor	4♭	b♭	e♭	a♭	d♭			
B♭ minor	5♭	b♭	e♭	a♭	d♭	g♭		
E♭ minor	6♭	b♭	e♭	a♭	d♭	g♭	c♭	
A♭ minor	7♭	b♭	e♭	a♭	d♭	g♭	c♭	f♭

You will notice in Figure 15.1 that, starting with A minor, we progressed up a perfect fifth to each new sharp key, and down a perfect fifth to each new flat key. This order is shown on the *circle of fifths for minor keys*.

Circle of Fifths for Minor Keys

The *circle of fifths for minor keys* is built exactly as its counterpart for major keys (p. 101). The key name for the key with no sharps or flats, A minor, is placed at the top of the circle. Sharp keys proceed clockwise and flat keys counterclockwise as shown in Figure 15.2. Notice the enharmonic keys of 5, 6, and 7 accidentals at the bottom of the circle, just as in major.

FIGURE 15.2 *The Circle of Fifths for Minor [1] Keys.*

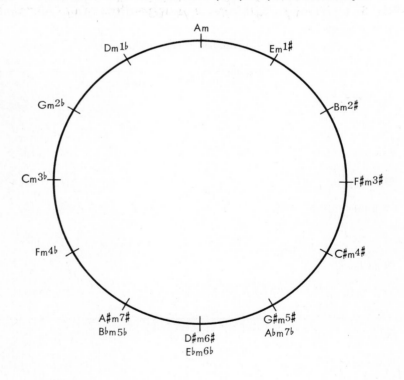

EXERCISES
15.1, 15.2,
15.3, 15.4,
15.5

1. The small letter *m* is used as an abbreviation for *minor*.

Minor Key Signatures on the Staff

The order of accidentals of the key signature on the staff is the same for minor as for major.

FIGURE 15.3 *Minor Key Signatures.*

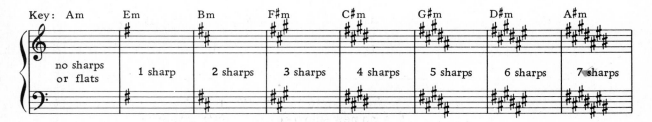

When it is known that the music is in a minor key, the number of sharps or flats in the signature will indicate the name of that minor key as shown in Figure 15.3. For example, when the key is minor, four sharps always indicate the key of C# minor.

EXERCISES
15.6, 15.7

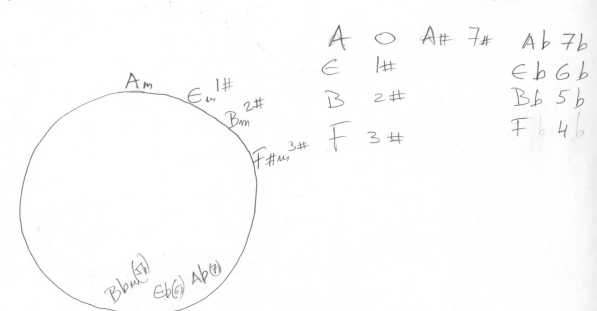

EXERCISE 15.1

Writing the numbers of accidentals for minor keys on the circle of fifths

On the circle of fifths below, the minor key names are given. Beside each key name, write the correct number of sharps or flats. The answer for E minor is given.

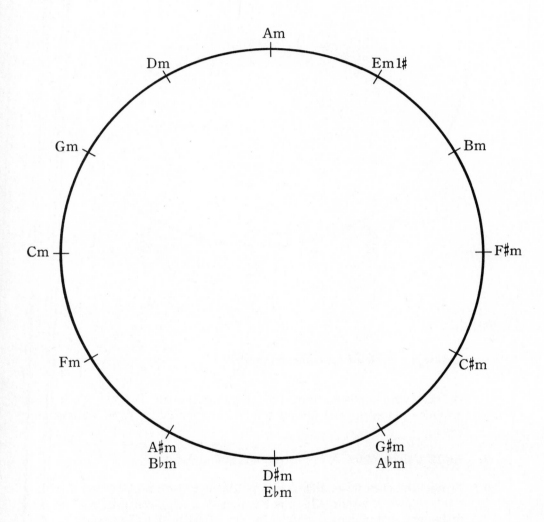

EXERCISE 15.2

Writing names of minor keys on the circle of fifths

On the circle below, the number of accidentals for each minor key signature is given. Beside each, write the name of the minor key. The answer for one flat is given.

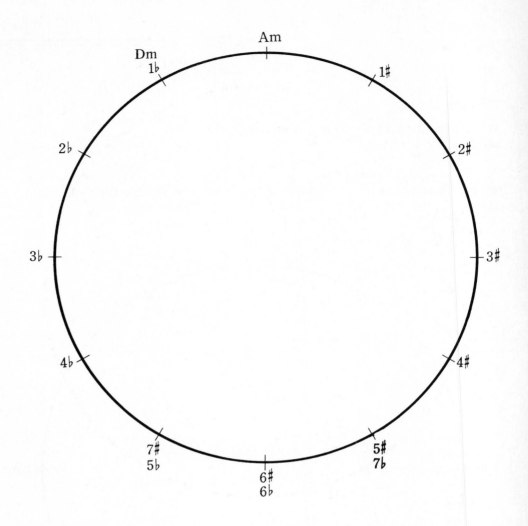

EXERCISE 15.3

Constructing the circle of fifths for minor keys

1. On the circle opposite, mark twelve points like the face of a clock. This provides places for all fifteen minor keys including three enharmonic keys.

2. At 12 o'clock place A minor (no sharps or flats).

3. Proceeding clockwise, at 1 o'clock place the letter name of the minor key a fifth above A minor, which is E minor (1 sharp); continue clockwise in fifths and add sharps through the key of A♯ minor (7 sharps).

4. Proceeding counterclockwise, at 11 o'clock place the letter name of the minor key a fifth below A minor, which is D minor (1♭); continue counter-clockwise in fifths and add flats through the key of A♭ minor (7 flats).

With practice, you should be able to reproduce the circle of fifths for minor keys (from memory) in *one minute*. Compare your results with Figure 15.2.

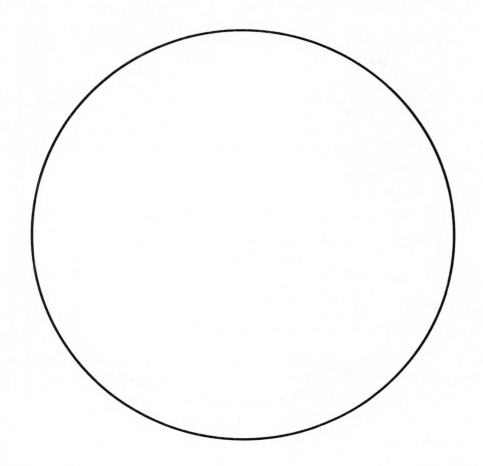

EXERCISE 15.4

Identifying minor key names from number of accidentals

In each blank space, write the correct minor key name according to the number of sharps or flats given.

(1) 2♯ _____ B minor _____   (8) 7♯ _____

(2) 4♭ _____   (9) 6♭ _____

(3) 3♭ _____   (10) 5♭ _____

(4) 5♯ _____   (11) 4♯ _____

(5) 1♯ _____   (12) 1♭ _____

(6) 7♭ _____   (13) 6♯ _____

(7) 3♯ _____   (14) 2♭ _____

EXERCISE 15.5

Naming the number of sharps or flats when the minor key is given

In each blank space, write the correct number of sharps or flats for the given minor key.

(1) B♭ minor _____ 5♭ _____   (8) G minor _____

(2) C♯ minor _____   (9) E minor _____

(3) A♭ minor _____   (10) F♯ minor _____ 3 ♯ _____

(4) G♯ minor _____ 5 ♯ _____   (11) F minor _____ 4♭ _____

(5) C minor _____ 3♭ _____   (12) B minor _____ 2 ♯ _____

(6) E♭ minor _____ 6 ♭ _____   (13) D♯ minor _____

(7) D minor _____ 1♭ _____   (14) A♯ minor _____ 7 ♯ _____

(*Return* to page *179*)

EXERCISE 15.6

Identifying name of minor key when key signature is given

For each key signature (1) write the name of the minor key below the staff, and (2) write the tonic note of the key on the staff, using a whole note.

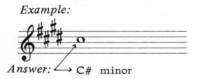

CHAPTER SIXTEEN

Major and Minor Key Relationships

The Circle of Fifths for Major and Minor Keys Together
Relative Keys
Parallel Keys
Solmization in Relative Major and Minor Keys

Although major and minor keys have been covered in two separate presentations, certain relationships exist between the two systems. The fact that there are seven sharp keys, seven flat keys, and one key without accidentals in each of major and minor is evidence that such a relationship exists. This evidence can be demonstrated graphically through further study of the circle of fifths.

The Circle of Fifths for Major and Minor Keys Together

We have already built one circle of fifths for major keys and another circle of fifths for minor keys. Each started with the key signature of no sharps or flats at the top of the circle and progressed clockwise by fifths up (sharp keys) and counterclockwise by fifths down (flat keys). This being so, we should be able to place major and minor keys in the same circle. Figure 16.1 shows such a circle, with the major keys outside the circle and minor keys inside the circle.

At each point in the circle are two keys that share the same accidentals (including the pairs at the bottom of the circle); these are known as *relative keys*.

Relative keys

A pair of keys, one major and one minor, located at the same point in the circle of fifths will each have the same accidentals and are known as *relative keys*. Each of these two relative keys will have identical signatures when placed on the staff.

The tonic of a minor key is the submediant tone of the relative major key, as shown in each illustration of relative keys in Figure 16.2. For example, the

FIGURE 16.1 *The Circle of Fifths for Major and Minor Keys Together.*

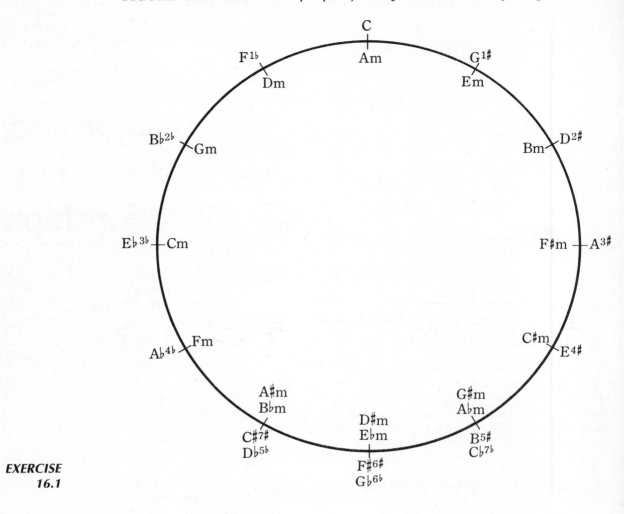

FIGURE 16.2 *Identical Signatures for Relative Major and Minor Keys.*

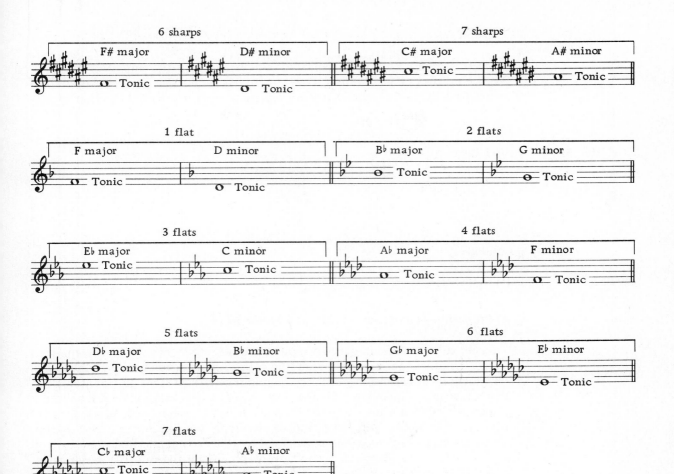

tonic of A minor is the submediant scale step of C major. The distance between these two tones is three half steps: this interval is called a *minor third*[1] (Figure 16.3*a*). The designation minor third will be used in the remainder of this discussion.

Notice that when a major tonic appears on a line, its relative minor tonic will be down a minor third, located on the next line. Similarly, when a major tonic appears on a space, its relative minor tonic will be down a minor third, located on the next space. See Figure 16.3*b, c*. (This may also be observed in Figure 16.2.)

FIGURE 16.3 *Locating Tonic Notes of Relative Keys.*

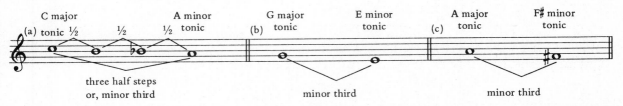

In an additional type of relationship, two keys are referred to as *parallel keys*.

EXERCISES
16.2, 16.3

1. In a minor third, the interval encompasses three letter names. Intervals will be studied in Chapters 17 and 18.

Parallel Keys

Parallel keys are keys with the same tonic note, but with completely different key signatures. For example, C major and C minor are parallel keys: they share C as tonic, but have different key signatures. Here are two other examples:

FIGURE 16.4 *Parallel Keys.*

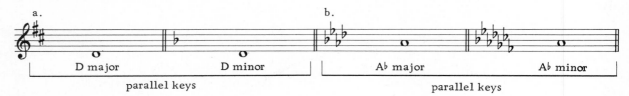

EXERCISE
16.4

Solmization in Relative Major and Minor Keys

Relationship between major and minor keys is further revealed in the application of syllables to the scales. When the system of the seven basic syllables was formulated, the intention was for *mi-fa* and *ti-do* to represent half steps and for any other pair of adjacent syllables to represent whole steps in both major and minor scale formations. In order for these pairs of syllables to coincide with their corresponding half steps and whole steps, the minor scale necessarily starts on *la,* as shown in Figure 16.5. Observe also that the first degree *do* of the major scale is identical to the third degree *do* of the relative minor scale and that the first degree *la* of the minor scale is identical to the sixth degree *la* of the relative major scale.

FIGURE 16.5 *The Syllabic Relationship Between Major and Minor Scales.*

C Major and Its Relative Key, A Minor.

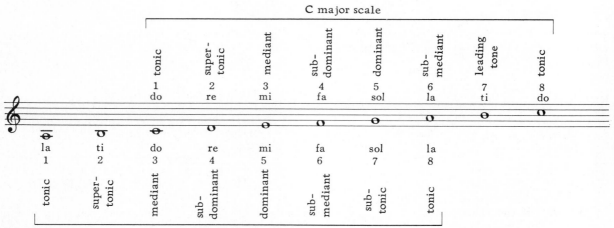

EXERCISE
16.5

For minor scales containing accidentals, the necessary syllables *fi* for raised 6 and *si* for raised 7 would be added.

EXERCISE 16.1

Constructing the circle of fifths for major and minor keys together

Place the major keys on the outside and the minor keys on the inside of the circle given.

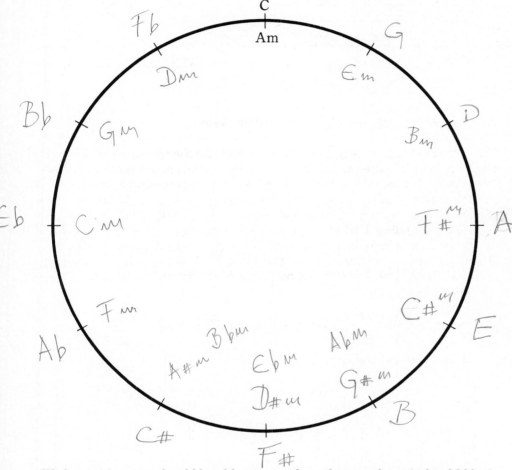

With practice, you should be able to reproduce the complete circle of fifths in less than *two minutes*. Compare your results with Figure 16.1.

(*Return* to page *188*)

EXERCISE 16.2

Identifying relative keys

Several procedures may be used to identify relative keys. Of those suggested below, the first is the easiest and quickest.

a) The relative key has the same key signature as the given key. Knowing the key name for this signature will provide the correct answer.

b) The relative minor key can be found a minor third below the tonic of a major key. The relative major key can be found a minor third above the tonic of a minor key.

c) Relative keys can readily be found on the circle of fifths.

Using any procedure, name the relative key for each of the following.

Example: given E♭ major   *Answer:*   <u>C minor</u>

(1)	C Major	_____
(2)	D Minor	_____
(3)	B Minor	<u>D MAJOR</u>
(4)	B♭ Major	_____
(5)	C♯ Minor	_____
(6)	F♯ Major	_____
(7)	G Minor	_____
(8)	A♭ Major	_____
(9)	A♭ Minor	_____
(10)	D Major	_____
(11)	F Major	_____
(12)	F♯ Minor	_____
(13)	A♯ Minor	_____
(14)	E Major	_____
(15)	D♯ Minor	_____
(16)	A Minor	_____
(17)	D♭ Major	_____
(18)	G♯ Minor	_____
(19)	E♭ Minor	_____
(20)	G Major	_____
(21)	G♭ Major	_____
(22)	B♭ Minor	_____
(23)	B Major	_____
(24)	C Minor	_____
(25)	C♭ Major	_____
(26)	E Minor	_____
(27)	C♯ Major	_____
(28)	F Minor	_____
(29)	A Major	_____

EXERCISE 16.3

Naming relative keys

Name the two keys, one major and one minor, indicated by the given key signature.

	Major Key	Minor Key
(1) 1 sharp	G Major	E Minor
(2) 4 flats		
(3) 3 sharps		
(4) none		
(5) 2 flats		
(6) 6 flats		
(7) 5 sharps		
(8) 2 sharps		
(9) 1 flat		
(10) 7 flats		
(11) 3 flats		
(12) 4 sharps		
(13) 6 sharps		
(14) 7 sharps		
(15) 5 flats		

(*Return* to page *189*)

EXERCISE 16.4

Naming key signatures of parallel keys

State the key signatures for both the major and minor keys which have the given pitch as tonic.

		Major	Minor
(1)	A♭	4♭	7♭
(2)	E		
(3)	F♯		
(4)	G		

193

(5)	C	_____	_____
(6)	E♭	_____	_____
(7)	C♯	_____	_____
(8)	B	_____	_____
(9)	D	_____	_____
(10)	A	_____	_____
(11)	F	_____	_____
(12)	B♭	_____	_____

(*Return* to page *190*)

EXERCISE 16.5

Solmization of major and minor scales

(a) Starting on any pitch as *do,* sing a major scale ascending and descending. Then sing down from *do* to *la* and sing the natural form of the relative minor scale.

(b) Starting on any pitch as *la,* sing the natural minor scale. Then, sing up from *la* to *do,* and sing the relative major scale.

CHAPTER SEVENTEEN

Intervals: Major and Perfect

Interval
Naming the Interval
Major and Perfect Intervals in the Major Scale
Analysis of Major and Perfect Intervals in the Major Scale
Simple and Compound Intervals

At various times in the preceding chapters we have had occasion to refer to *intervals;* the term itself was identified as early as Chapter Two, page 18. We have used intervals of the half step, the whole step, and the octave to help us in constructing the scale, the perfect fifth to help us understand the circle of fifths, and the minor third for locating relative keys. We will now make a more complete study beginning with a review of the definition of the term *interval*.

Interval

An *interval* is the distance or difference between two pitches. A *harmonic interval* is the sounding of two pitches simultaneously; a *melodic interval* is the sounding of two pitches consecutively.

FIGURE 17.1 *Harmonic and Melodic Intervals.*

harmonic
interval

melodic interval
ascending

melodic interval
descending

Since any combination of two different pitches will produce an interval, it follows that many different types of intervals exist, requiring a system for *naming intervals*.

The name of an interval always consists of two parts:

1. A noun describing its *quantity,* that is, the numerical distance between its two pitches, or, on the staff, between its two notes. By counting the number of lines and spaces or the number of letter names encompassed, the quantity of an interval is established. For example, the interval from G up to B is a third because it encompasses three lines and spaces, and also encompasses three letter names.

FIGURE 17.2 *The Quantity of an Interval.*

The possible names that indicate quantity are: *prime, second, third, fourth, fifth, sixth, seventh,* and *octave.*[1]

2. An adjective describing its *quality,* that is, the difference in the characteristics of two intervals that encompass the same number of lines and spaces, or of letter names, but which have a different number of half steps. For example, both of the intervals G up to B and G up to B♭ encompass three letter names, but G up to B encompasses four half steps while G up to B♭ encompasses only three half steps.

FIGURE 17.3 *Differences in Interval Quality.*

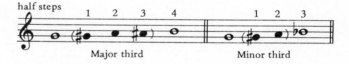

The possible names that describe quality are: *major, minor, perfect, diminished,* and *augmented.* Every interval is described by a combination of terms indicating both its quantity and its quality, such as major third, perfect fifth, and so forth. These are the possible combinations:

major and minor[2]	refer only to	seconds, thirds, sixths, and sevenths
perfect[2]	refers only to	fourths, fifths, and octaves
diminished and augmented	refer to	any interval

1. Larger intervals are *compound* intervals. See page 199.
2. The terms *major* (this chapter) and *minor* (next chapter) when applied to intervals simply mean larger (greater) or smaller (lesser). For an explanation of "perfect," see footnote 8 on page 226.

Other combinations, such as "major fourth" or "perfect third," do not exist.

We will begin our study of intervals with those found above the tonic tone of a major scale.

Major and Perfect Intervals in the Major Scale

In a major scale, distance from the tonic note up to each of the other scale tones provides seven different intervals. These, with their interval names, are:

from scale degree	up to scale degree	the interval name is	abbreviated
1	2	Major Second or whole step	M2 *two ½ steps* 2
1	3	Major Third	M3 *4 ½ steps* 4
1	4	Perfect Fourth	P4 *five ½ steps* 5
1	5	Perfect Fifth	P5 *Seven ½ steps* 7
1	6	Major Sixth	M6 *9 ½ steps* 9
1	7	Major Seventh	M7 *11 ½ steps* 11
1	8	Perfect Octave	P8 *12 ½ steps* 12
1	1	Perfect Prime or Unison[3]	P1 (PP)

FIGURE 17.4 *Intervals in the C Major Scale.*

These intervals are found in the same order in any major scale, for example, D major.

FIGURE 17.5 *Intervals in the D Major Scale.*

3. The perfect prime, while not an interval by previous definition, is the name given to two notes of the same pitch. When both pitches sound together (for example, a soprano and an alto singing the same pitch), the PP is commonly called a *unison*.

FIGURE 17.6 *Specific Major and Perfect Intervals in the Major Scale.*

Major Intervals		Perfect Intervals	
Name	Scale Steps	Name	Scale Steps
M2	1 — 2	P4	1 — 4
M3	1 — 3	P5	1 — 5
M6	1 — 6	P8	1 — 8
M7	1 — 7		

Other intervals which will be studied later use the adjectives *minor, diminished* and *augmented.* However, in the major scale only major and perfect intervals occur above the tonic note.

Analysis of Major and Perfect Intervals in the Major Scale

In analyzing an interval, assume the lower note to be 1 (tonic) and count the scale degrees to the upper note. The number of scale degrees will determine the name of the interval. For example, D up to A:

A appears as the fifth degree in the D major scale; therefore, D up to A is a perfect fifth.

Also, B♭ up to G:

G appears as the sixth degree in the B♭ major scale; therefore B♭ up to G is a major sixth.

This procedure for analysis, where the lower note is assumed to be 1, is the same for harmonic intervals. For example, G and B:

B appears as the third degree in the G major scale; therefore, the interval is a major third.

The procedure is the same for descending melodic intervals. Calculate from the lower note of the interval. For example, to determine the name of the interval A down to E, calculate from E, the lower note, up to A.

A appears as the fourth degree in the E major scale and A up to E is a perfect fourth. A down to E is, of course, the same interval as E up to A, therefore, A down to E is a perfect fourth.

The intervals shown in this chapter, as well as all other intervals, can be found in both *simple* and *compound* forms.

Simple and Compound Intervals

Intervals encompassing a perfect octave or less are known as *simple* intervals. Intervals larger than a perfect octave are called *compound* intervals because they are made up of an octave plus a *simple* interval, already named. Like simple intervals, compound intervals are designated by the number of scale degrees spanned.

FIGURE 17.7 *Simple and Compound Intervals in the C Major Scale.*

When two intervals are added together, as shown for the major ninth, the intervallic sum is always one number less than the arithmetical sum:

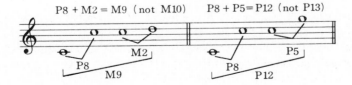

In musical analysis, compound intervals are frequently reduced to simple terminology. For example, although the interval C to G, P8 + P5, is a perfect twelfth, it may be called a perfect fifth.

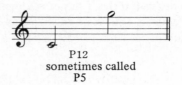

P12
sometimes called
P5

EXERCISE 17.1

Naming intervals found above the tonic in the major scale

The first note or lower note of each measure is the tonic of the scale. In parts (a) and (b) the intervals are found in ascending order. In parts (c), (d) and (e) the intervals are ascending in random order. In part (f) the intervals are descending; the lower note is the tonic of the scale.

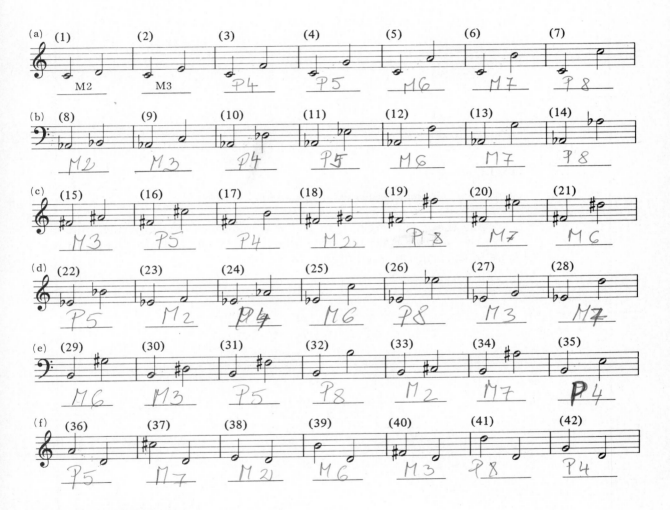

(*Return* to page *198*)

EXERCISE 17.2

Analyzing major and perfect intervals

Identify interval by name. Write abbreviation below each interval given.

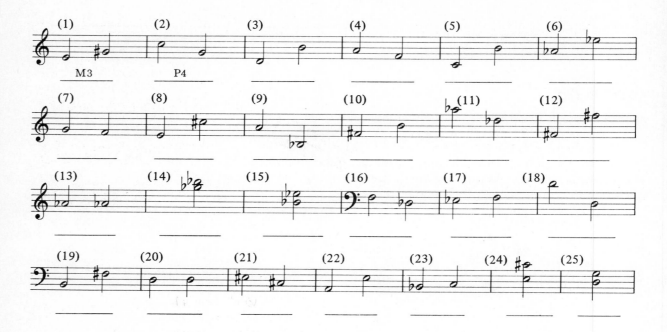

(*Return* to page *199*)

EXERCISE 17.3

Analyzing compound intervals (major and perfect only)

Name the given interval. In the blank measure following each interval, write the simple form of the given interval and identify it by its name. Either note of the original interval may be moved.

CHAPTER EIGHTEEN

Intervals
(continued)

Homework [handwritten]

Minor Intervals
Diminished Intervals
Augmented Intervals
Modification of Intervals
Analysis of Intervals
~~**Intervals in Inversion**~~

In the previous chapter, we measured the distance of each note of the major scale from the tonic and obtained either major or perfect intervals. Three other types of intervals also exist in music; none of these is found as an interval above the tonic of the major scale. To measure these new intervals, each will be compared to the major and perfect intervals already studied. These new intervals are:

minor (abbr. *m.* or *min.*)
diminished (abbr. *dim.* or sometimes °)
augmented (abbr. *aug.* or sometimes +)

Minor Intervals

A *minor* interval is one half step smaller than a major interval. Figure 18.1, in column 3, shows that minor intervals are one half step smaller than the major intervals of column 1.

Diminished Intervals

A diminished interval is one half step smaller than a perfect interval (compare column 4 with column 2 in Figure 18.1) and also is one half step smaller than a minor interval (compare column 4 with column 3). By comparing column 4 with column 1, it will be seen that diminished intervals are one whole step smaller than major intervals.

FIGURE 18.1 *Intervals Above C.*

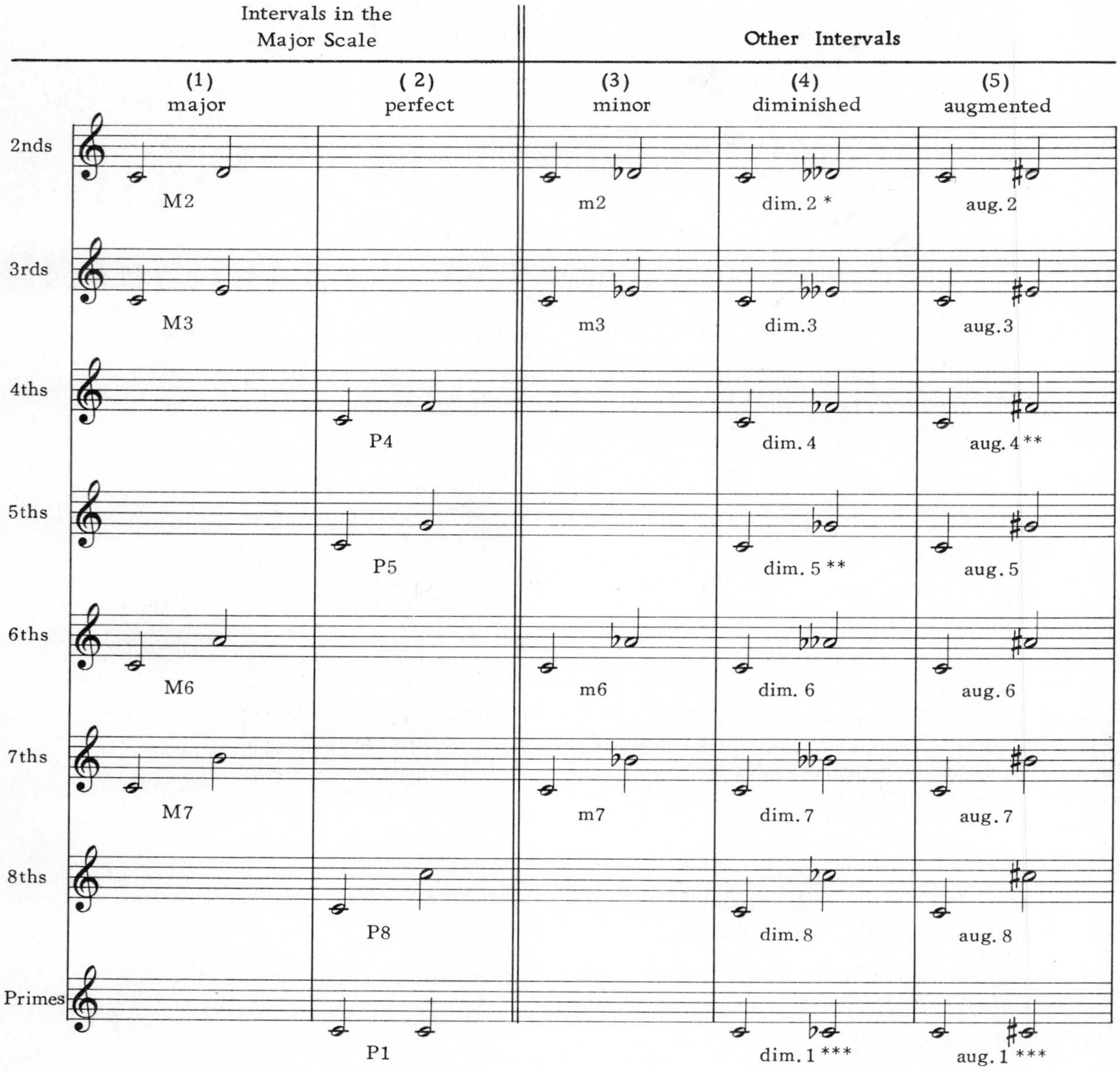

| | Intervals in the Major Scale | | Other Intervals | | |
	(1) major	(2) perfect	(3) minor	(4) diminished	(5) augmented
2nds	M2		m2	dim. 2 *	aug. 2
3rds	M3		m3	dim. 3	aug. 3
4ths		P4		dim. 4	aug. 4 **
5ths		P5		dim. 5 **	aug. 5
6ths	M6		m6	dim. 6	aug. 6
7ths	M7		m7	dim. 7	aug. 7
8ths		P8		dim. 8	aug. 8
Primes		P1		dim. 1 ***	aug. 1 ***

*Enharmonic with the Perfect Prime (C — C = C — D♭♭)

**Also called *tritone*. The dim. 5 and aug. 4 each encompass *three whole steps* and thus are enharmonic with each other.

***Usually called a *chromatic half step*. As a dim. prime, the second note is lower than the first note.

Augmented Intervals

The augmented interval is one half step larger than a perfect interval (compare column 5 with column 2) and also is one half step larger than a major interval (compare column 5 with column 1).

Modification of Intervals

In Figure 18.1, it can be seen that any type of interval (M, m, P, dim., or aug.) is a modification by one half step of some other type of interval. This is shown in Figure 18.2.

FIGURE 18.2 *Modification of Intervals.*

Type of Interval Before	Modification		Type of Interval After
M	− ½ step	=	m
m	− ½ step	=	dim.
P	− ½ step	=	dim.
dim.	− ½ step	=	(doubly dim.)[1]
aug.	− ½ step	=	P or M
M	+ ½ step	=	aug.
m	+ ½ step	=	M
P	+ ½ step	=	aug.
dim.	+ ½ step	=	P or m
aug.	+ ½ step	=	(doubly aug.)[1]

When modifying an interval as shown in Figure 18.2, the half step in each instance is a *chromatic half step,* that is, a half step using the *same letter name.* Thus, in Figure 18.1, when the M3, C up to E is modified to become a m3 (M3 minus ½ step = m3), the half step E to E♭ is used. Lowering the E to D♯ produces the interval C–D♯ which is an augmented second, since only two letter names are encompassed.

Modification by half step may be applied to *either* the upper note *or* the lower note of an interval. The major third C up to E becomes the minor third C♯ up to E when the lower note is raised one half step *using the same letter name,* thereby reducing the major third by one half step.

EXERCISE 18.1

1. Doubly diminished and doubly augmented intervals are uncommon in musical practice and will not be considered further in this text.

Analysis of Intervals

To analyze, identify, and write any interval, your knowledge of intervals from Chapter 17 and the information from Figures 18.1 and 18.2 will suffice.

1. When the Lower Note of an Interval Is Tonic of a Major Scale

Whether the interval to be identified is ascending or descending, first locate the lower note of the interval (either the first or the second note), assume it to be tonic (1) of a major scale, and count the scale degrees to the upper note. If the upper note appears in the major scale, it is either a *major* or a *perfect* interval. If the upper note does not belong to the major scale then it is a *minor*, a *diminished*, or an *augmented* interval, according to its alteration as shown in Figure 18.1.

For example, consider the interval G up to E♭: G up to E would be a M6; therefore G up to E♭, a decrease of one half step, is a m6.

M6   decrease by 1/2 step
                    m6

Analyze the interval B up to F×; B up to F♯ would be a perfect fifth; therefore B up to F×, an increase of one half step, is an aug. 5. Observe that F♯ was raised to F×, which uses the *same letter name,* rather than to its enharmonic equivalent, G, which would have been a minor sixth.

P5   increase by 1/2 step
                    aug. 5

Analyze the interval A♯ down to E; since E is the lower note, count up the E major scale to A, a P4; A♯ is an increase of one half step, therefore E up to A♯, or A♯ down to E, is an augmented fourth.

calculate
from this note
↓

P4   increase by 1/2 step
                    aug. 4

EXERCISE 18.2

To write an interval above a given note, use the same process applied in analyzing an interval. For example, to write a minor sixth above F, consider F

2. In scales with a key signature of four or more flats, some of the intervals in column 4 (dim.) would require a "triple flat" (♭♭♭), e.g., G♭ up to B♭♭♭. This type of notation is impractical. If such an interval were needed in actual music (and this would be rare), it would be spelled enharmonically.

as the tonic of F major and count up six scale steps to D. F up to D is a major sixth, so by lowering D one half step to D♭, you have F up to D♭, which is a minor sixth.

EXERCISE
18.3

2. Identifying Any Interval (P, M, m, dim., aug.) *When the Lower Note Is Not the Tonic of a Major Scale.*

By changing the ♯ or ♭ of the lower note to natural (♮), we can easily find an interval based on the lower note as tonic of a major scale. By replacing the ♯ or ♭ and observing the increase or decrease in the size of the interval, according to Figure 18.2, the name of the original interval will become apparent. Consider the interval D♯ up to A: D natural up to A would be a P5; therefore D♯ up to A, a decrease by a half step, is a dim.5.

Consider F♭ up to B♭: since there is no scale of F♭, calculate the interval from F natural up to B♭, a P4; therefore, F♭ up to B♭, an increase by a half step, is an aug.4.

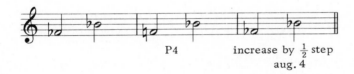

The analysis of a few uncommon spellings of intervals may be more complex:

The student's power of reasoning, however, might supply a simpler solution: since D to F♯ is a M3, then D♯ to F×, with both notes raised a half step is also a M3.

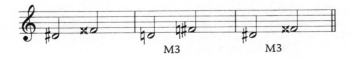

EXERCISE
18.4

To write an interval above a given note, use the same process, for example, a dim.5 above F♭:

1. change F♭ to F♮
2. in the scale of F major, F up to C is a P5
3. a dim.5 above F is C♭
4. lower both notes of F–C♭ to F♭–C♭♭

Enharmonic intervals are frequently obvious, especially when related to the keyboard. In fact, any diminished or augmented interval is enharmonic with some perfect, major, or minor interval, except the diminished fifth and the augmented fourth (tritone) which are enharmonic with each other. For example, C up to G♯ is an aug.5 and C up to A♭ is a m6; G♯ and A♭ are enharmonic and are the same key on the keyboard. Caution is due in this respect: proper spellings must be maintained according to the designation of the interval. It is incorrect to say that C up to G♯ is a m6 or that C up to A♭ is an aug.5 even though the intervals are enharmonic.

FIGURE 18.3 *Enharmonic Intervals.*

EXERCISES 18.5, 18.6, 18.7

Intervals in Inversion

You may have noticed that some pairs of intervals use the same pitch names, yet look and sound different from the other pair. The notes D and F♯, for example, can be used as D up to F♯, a major third, or F♯ up to D, a minor sixth (the same is true when the notes are descending).

Each of the two intervals in this relationship is said to be an *inversion* of the other. An interval can be inverted when its lower note is placed one octave

FIGURE 18.4 *Inverting an Interval.*

(a) moving the lower tone up an octave

(b) moving the upper tone down an octave

M3   m6

higher, or its upper note one octave lower. In either case, there is a change in size of the interval but no change in the pitch names used.[3]

Any interval built on any pitch can be inverted by this process, as seen in Figure 18.5, where, for illustration, the C is the lower note in each interval and is placed an octave higher in the inversion.

FIGURE 18.5 *Inversions on the Staff.*

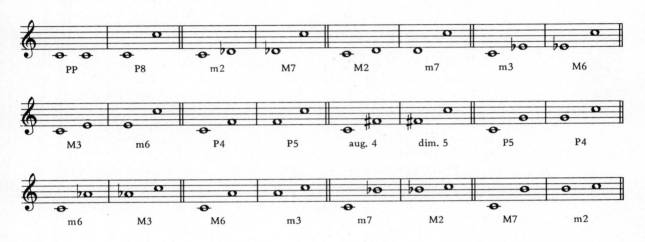

FIGURE 18.6 *Table of Inversions.*

Interval	Inversion	Interval	Inversion
PP	P8	dim. 5	aug. 4
m2	M7	P5	P4
M2	m7	aug. 5	dim. 4
aug. 2	dim. 7	m6	M3
dim. 3	aug. 6	M6	m3
m3	M6	aug. 6	dim. 3
M3	m6	dim. 7	aug. 2
dim. 4	aug. 5	m7	M2
P4	P5	M7	m2
aug. 4	dim. 5	P8	PP

3. Jean Phillipe Rameau, theorist and composer, noted in 1722 that any pitch and its octave sounded the same except that one was an octave higher. Therefore, he reasoned, one note of the octave represents the other, and in that sense, one is the same as the other. Thus, an interval differing from another interval only by octave transposition of one note is merely a different expression of the same sound.

Observe in Figures 18.5 and 18.6 that:

a *perfect* interval inverts to a *perfect* interval
a *minor* interval inverts to a *major* interval
a *major* interval inverts to a *minor* interval
a *diminished* interval inverts to an *augmented* interval
an *augmented* interval inverts to a *diminished* interval

HOMEWORK
P-184
P-192
P-193
P-194
P-202
P-211-213

NAME _____

EXERCISE 18.1

Modification of intervals

a) Major to minor. Supply the second note of the minor interval as indicated. For this exercise (all parts, *a-e*) use a natural sign ♮ if the second note is natural. Use half notes.

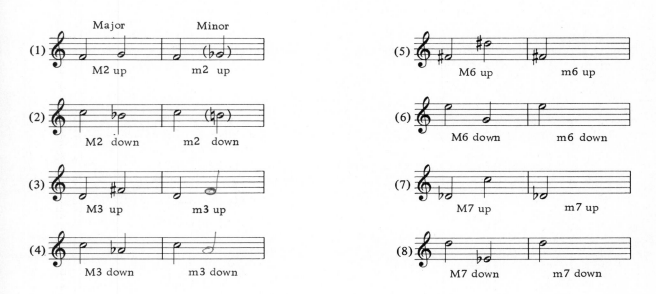

b) Minor to diminished. Supply the second note of each diminished interval as directed. Use half notes.

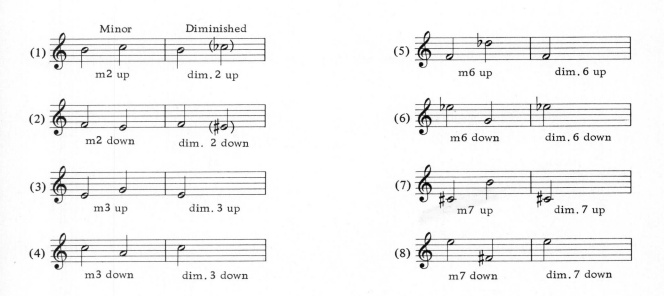

c) Perfect to diminished. Supply the second note of each diminished interval.
Use half notes.

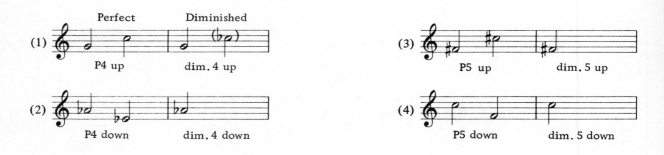

d) Major to augmented. Supply the second note of each augmented interval.
Use half notes.

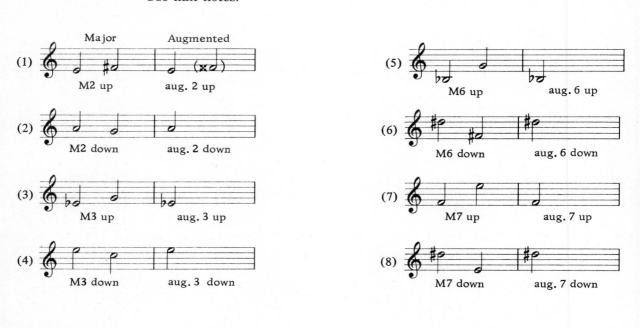

e) Perfect to augmented. Supply the second note of each augmented interval.
Use half notes.

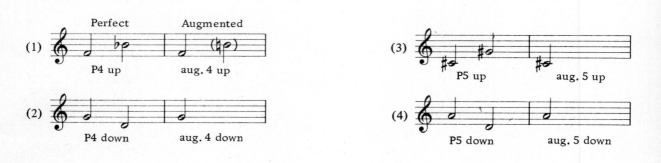

(*Return* to page 206)

EXERCISE 18.2

Analyzing minor, diminished, and augmented intervals.

Below each interval, write the interval name.

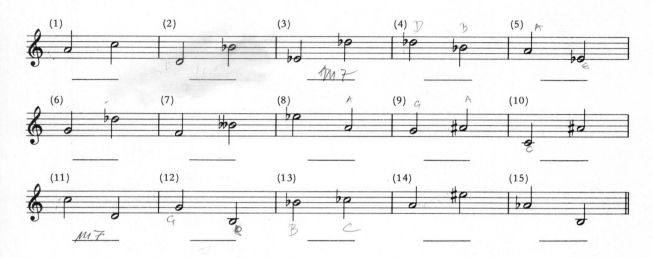

(*Return* to page 206)

EXERCISE 18.3

Writing minor, diminished, and augmented intervals

Write on the staff the second note of these ascending intervals. Use half notes.

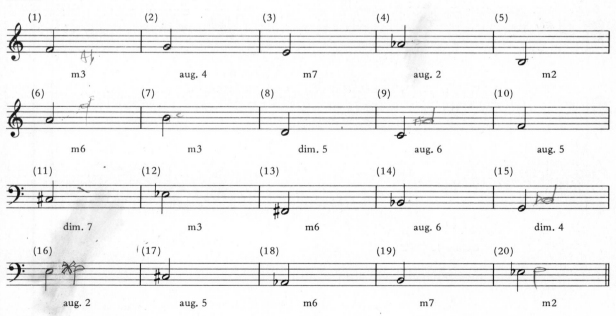

(*Return* to page 207)

EXERCISE 18.4

Analyzing all types of intervals above notes which cannot be tonics of major scales

Below each interval write the interval name.

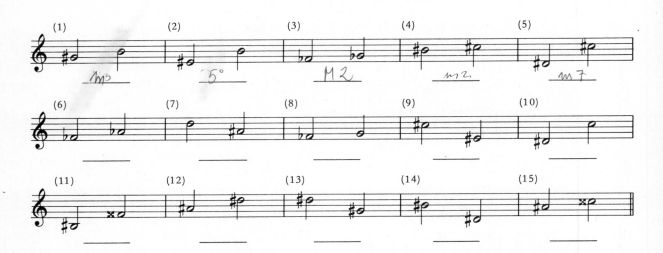

(*Return* to page 208)

EXERCISE 18.5

Writing intervals above notes which cannot be tonics of major scales

Write on the staff the second note of these ascending intervals. Use half notes.

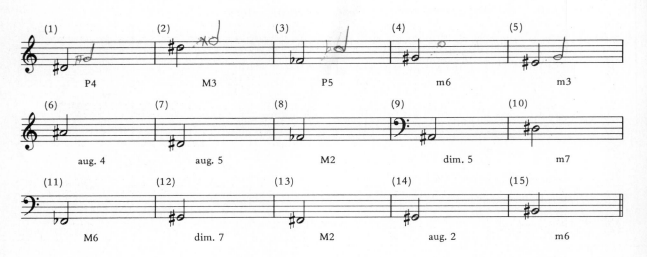

EXERCISE 18.6

Analyzing all types of intervals

Identify interval by name. Write abbreviation below each interval given.

EXERCISE 18.7

Spelling all types of intervals

Write the letter name of the second note of each interval given.

Example: m3 above D♯ is ___F♯___

(1) M3 above B is _____

(2) Dim. 5 above A is _____

(3) P8 above E♯ is _____

(4) m7 above G is _____

(5) Aug. 2 above G is _____

(6) P4 above F♯ is _____

(7) Dim. 7 above F♯ is _____

(8) P5 above D♯ is _____

(9) M2 above G♭ is _____

(10) M6 above C♯ is _____

(11) P4 above F♯ is _____

(12) M7 above E is _____

(13) Aug. 6 above B♭ is _____

(14) m2 above C♯ is _____

(15) m6 above D is _____

(16) Aug. 5 above E is _____

(17) m3 above D♭ is _____

(18) M3 above G is _____

(19) Aug. 4 above F is _____

(20) m6 above F is _____

(21) Dim. 4 above E♭ is _____

(22) m3 above A is _____

(23) Aug. 2 above E is _____

(24) P5 above G♭ is _____

(25) Dim. 3 above E♭ is _____

(*Return* to page *208*)

EXERCISE 18.8

Inversion of intervals

Name the inversion of each of these intervals.

(1) Perfect fifth   _____

(2) Major second   _____

(3) Minor sixth   _____

(4) Major third   _____

(5) Augmented fourth   _____

(6) Minor second   _____

(7) Major sixth   _____

(8) Minor seventh   _____

(9) Minor third   _____

(10) Perfect fourth   _____

(11) Diminished fifth   _____

(12) Major sixth   _____

EXERCISE 18.9

Inversion of intervals

Place on the staff the inversion of the given interval and state the name of both intervals. Write the inversion of each given interval in two ways:

(1)   move the upper note down an octave, and
(2)   move the lower note up an octave (in either order).

Harmony I: Chords; Major Triads

The term *harmony* refers to the simultaneous sounding of two or more pitches. Music in Western culture, especially since about the year 1600, is based to a great extent on the principles of harmony. We have already experienced a simple form of harmony in *harmonic intervals* (page 195) where the two tones of the interval sound together. When three or more tones sound together, the result is a *chord*.

Chords

Chords are usually built using intervals of the major and minor third.[1] A chord structure is most easily demonstrated when, like a harmonic interval, the notes of the chord are placed on the staff in vertical alignment, indicating that all tones sound simultaneously. This configuration is known as a *block chord*. Figure 19.1 shows at (1) a single tone, followed by harmonic structures above that tone: at (2) an interval, and at (3), (4), and (5), three varieties of chords.

FIGURE 19.1 *Harmonic Structures*.

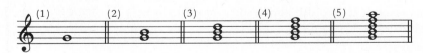

1. This is generally true of music written before the twentieth century. Chords built in thirds are known as *tertian harmony*. Later practice has added chords built in seconds, fourths (quartal harmony), and fifths (quintal harmony).

Chord tones also may sound successively; in this form chords are known as *broken chords* or *arpeggiated chords,* in contrast to the block chords shown in Figure 19.1. When appearing as a left-hand accompaniment to a melody on the piano (Figure 19.2*b*), the series of broken chords is often known as an *Alberti bass,* named after Domenico Alberti (1710-1740) who was one of the first composers to use the device extensively.

FIGURE 19.2 *Broken Chords; Alberti Bass.*

Our study of harmony will focus on the three-note chord, Figure 19.1 (3), a sonority known as a *triad.*

The Triad

The triad is a very commonly used structure in harmonic music.[2] It consists of two consecutive intervals of the third above a given note, and can easily be built on the staff using three consecutive lines, Figure 19.3*a*, or three consecutive spaces, Figure 19.3*b*.

FIGURE 19.3 *Building a Triad.*

EXERCISE 19.1

The lowest note of the triad (the note upon which the triad is built) is known as the *root* of the triad. The note immediately above the root is the *third,* since it is at the interval of a third above the root. The remaining note is the *fifth* of the triad since it is a fifth above the root. The three triad members may also be referred to as 1, 3, and 5.

2. The triad is also used in the construction of more complex chords such as those in Figure 19.1 at (4) and (5). These are not included in the scope of this book with the exception of the structure at (4), presented on page 219.

FIGURE 19.4 *Triad Members*.

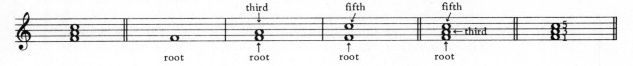

EXERCISE
19.2

Although all triads have a root, third, and a fifth, there are several *types of triads*.

Types of Triads

If we write a triad above each of the seven letters of the musical alphabet, we produce the seven basic triad spellings (those without sharps or flats).

FIGURE 19.5 *Basic Triad Spellings*.

When these are played on the piano and we listen carefully to each, we will discover that some sound like others even though located at different pitch levels. This is because those which sound the same display the same arrangement of major and minor thirds within the triad.

There are four combinations of major and minor thirds; each combination produces a different type of triad with its own identifying name.

Figure 19.5 indicates the first three of these types.

1. major triad: C E G, F A C, and G B D
2. minor triad: D F A, E G B, and A C E
3. diminished triad: B D F
4. augmented triad: requires the use of an accidental, as in C E G#.

We will investigate each of these triads in the above order, beginning in this chapter with the *major triad*.

The Major Triad

In the major triad, the arrangement of intervals above the lowest note is major third and minor third, while the distance from the root up to the fifth is a perfect fifth.

FIGURE 19.6 *The Major Triad on C*.

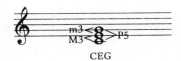

Any pitch name can serve as the root of a major triad. The most commonly used major triads are those whose roots have the same pitch names as the tonic tones of the 15 major scales, which were studied in Chapter 4. If you can spell these scales, you can quickly spell major triads based on their tonic notes simply by selecting steps 1, 3, and 5 of the scale, for example:

Major key	Scale steps 1, 3, 5		
F	F	A	C
E♭	E♭	G	B♭
A	A	C♯	E

EXERCISE 19.3

Each of the remaining possible major triad spellings has as its root a chromatic tone.[3] Any such triad, including those described in the preceding paragraph, can easily be spelled by a single method.

1. When the root carries a sharp (♯), lower the sharp to a natural (♮), spell the triad on that pitch, and then raise all pitch names one half step.

   Problem: Spell a major triad on D♯
   Solution: Spell a major triad on D: D F♯ A
   Raise all notes one half step: D♯ F✕ A♯

2. When the root carries a flat (♭) or a double flat (♭♭), raise the accidental one half step, ♭ to ♮, or ♭♭ to ♭, spell the major triad on that pitch, and then lower all notes one half step.

   Problem: Spell a major triad on D♭♭
   Solution: Spell a major triad on D♭: D♭ F A♭
   Lower all notes one half step: D♭♭ F♭ A♭♭

EXERCISE 19.4

If you are fluent in spelling intervals, it is often easier simply to spell any major triad by its intervallic structure. For example, to spell a major triad above A♭:

$$M3 + m3 = A♭\text{-}C + C\text{-}E♭ = A♭\ C\ E♭$$

or,

$$M3 \text{ and } P5 = A♭\text{-}C + A♭\text{-}E♭ = A♭\ C\ E♭$$

EXERCISE 19.5

3. Raising or lowering a basic letter name a half step using an accidental (♯, ♭, etc.) produces a chromatic tone, such as D to D♯. Triads built on chromatic notes, other than those built on the tonics of major or minor scales, range in frequency of use from moderate to rare.

Up to this point we have considered the triad only when the root is the lowest note. Rearranging the notes of the triad so that the third or fifth is the lowest note results in *inversion of the triad.*

Inversion of Triads[4]

When either the third or the fifth of any triad is found as the lowest note, the triad is said to be in *inversion,* or, put in a slightly different way, the triad is *inverted. First inversion* indicates that the third of the triad is the lowest note, while *second inversion* indicates that the fifth of the triad is the lowest note.

FIGURE 19.7 *Inversions of the C Major Triad.*

Notice that intervals which are not found in the root position of the triad appear between triad members in inversion.

FIGURE 19.8 *Intervals in Inverted Triads.*

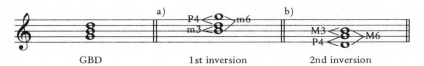

These inversions do not alter the identification of the triad. When the three tones of the inverted triad are rearranged in thirds, the lowest note of these thirds is always the root. In Figure 19.8*a*, although the first inversion reads B D G from the lowest note up, these notes can be rearranged in thirds to become G B D; likewise in Figure 19.8*b*, D G B is recognized as a G B D triad.[5]

EXERCISE 19.6

In addition to variation by inversion, triads can also be varied by *position.*

4. The discussion in this section and the following two sections (*triad position* and *doubling*) apply equally to all types of chords.

5. Inversion of triads is based on the same principle as inversion of intervals (review footnote 3, page 209). When the lowest note of the triad is placed an octave higher, this octave represents the original note, and the triad remains unchanged except for the arrangement of its members.

Prior to Rameau's theory (1722), analysis of vertical sonorities was based solely on the intervals above the lowest note. Thus the three triads in Figure 19.8 were considered three different sonorities.

Triad Position

Any triad (or any other chord) whose notes are as close together on the staff as possible is said to be in *close position*. In *open position* the tones are placed further apart from each other. You can easily recognize a chord in open position because there will be one or more places in its structure where a chord member could have been inserted.

FIGURE 19.9 *Close and Open Position.*[6]

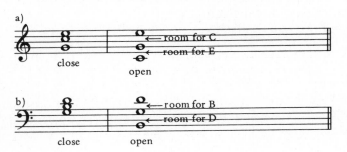

EXERCISE 19.7

An additional way of varying a triad is through *doubling* of any of its members.

Doubling

In almost all composed music, more than three notes sound simultaneously. Therefore, when a triad is used, one or more of its notes must be *doubled;* that is, a given pitch spelling will be used two or more times.

FIGURE 19.10 *Doubled Tones.*

Doubling is most frequent when the great staff is used. Figure 19.11 shows a series of triads, each written using four notes, requiring one note in each triad to be doubled.

FIGURE 19.11 *Doubling in Triads on the Great Staff.*

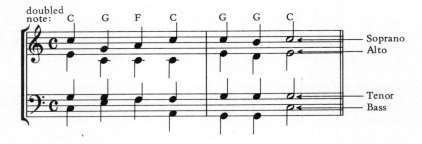

EXERCISE 19.8

6. Also called close/open structure; close/open harmony; close/open voicing.

Figure 19.11 is written in the *four-part* (or *four-voice*) *chorale* style that is commonly used in church hymns and in patriotic and community songs, such as *America* and *Auld Lang Syne*. The names of the four voices are indicated at the right of the figure. Each person performs his or her part by reading from left to right, guided (in Figure 19.11) by the stem direction on the notes of each part; soprano, stems up; alto, stems down; tenor, stems up; bass, stems down.

This example demonstrates with extreme simplicity the dual concept basic to music composition in the period c.1600-c.1900, as well as much of the music of the twentieth century. The horizontal aspect of music composition is the sounding of melodic lines[7] (sometimes several simultaneously as in Figure 19.11). The vertical aspect is the harmonic structure (chords) at any point, and the use of these chords in succession. Both the horizontal and the vertical aspects are of equal importance, and special skills are required to combine them successfully; these are presented in more advanced studies in Harmony.

We have seen in the preceding material a number of ways in which triads are used, all illustrated with abstract examples. When we look at most any example of "real" music, we will find the use of one additional feature that is not part of the triad itself; this is *dissonance*.

Dissonance and Consonance

Looking at the next example, Figure 19.12, we see a simple folk song with an accompaniment of only two triads, G B D and D F♯ A (the D F♯ A C chord will be discussed shortly). Measure 1 shows a triad, G B D, and, in the melody, another pitch, A (circled), that is not part of the triad. The pitch A as used here is an example of *dissonance,* in contrast to the *consonance,* G B D, with which it sounds. In the example, other dissonances are also circled.

FIGURE 19.12 *Harmony with Dissonance.*

Traditionally, *consonance* refers to a pleasant sound while *dissonance* refers to a harsh or unpleasant sound. For the present purpose of definition, a harmony is consonant when it contains only those intervals found in a triad and

---

7. The simultaneous sounding of two or more melodic lines, usually displaying more melodic and rhythmic contrast than shown here, is known as *counterpoint*.

its inversions.[8] Any additional tone sounding simultaneously with the triad is therefore dissonant to that triad.

Music written early in the history of the art (c. 1000 A.D.) used dissonance sparingly. The history of music is, in part, a history of the increasing use of dissonance and the increased tolerance of the ear for such sounds. The words "consonance" and "dissonance" are used today only as identifying terms; they do not necessarily describe the effect of any sound upon any particular listener.

Dissonant tones may be found in one of two ways:

1. The *nonharmonic tone.* Any tone that is not part of a triad but that sounds simultaneously with it, except as in "2" below, is known as a *nonharmonic tone.*[9] In Figure 19.12, each circled note in the melody is not part of the triad with which it sounds. Each is therefore dissonant and identified as a nonharmonic tone.

2. The *seventh chord.* In the next-to-the-last measure of Figure 19.12, we see the chord spelling D F♯ A C. Here, the pitch C is an additional third placed above the major triad D F♯ A. D F♯ A C is a chord because it is built in thirds, but it is dissonant because it contains the dissonant interval of a minor seventh, D up to C, shown in Figure 19.13. With this particular arrangement of thirds, the chord is known as a major-minor seventh chord (major triad plus interval of a minor seventh).

FIGURE 19.13 *The Seventh Chord.*

Like triads, seventh chords can be inverted. Since the seventh chord is a four-note chord, there are three inversions.

FIGURE 19.14 *Inversions of a Seventh Chord.*

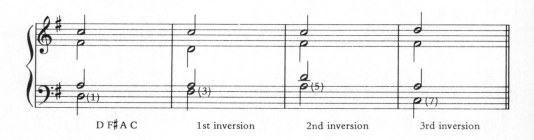

8. These are: major and minor thirds, major and minor sixths, the perfect fourth, the perfect fifth, and the octave. Of the consonant intervals, those that cannot in any context suggest a major or minor key are called *perfect.*

9. Some of the other names in current usage are: non-chord tones, foreign tones, accessory tones, and bytones. Nonharmonic tones can be identified and named more specifically based on the way they are approached and left in the melodic line, and are described in most harmony texts. In Ottman, *Elementary Harmony,* see pages 219–228.

Figure 19.15 shows nonharmonic tones (circled) and seventh chords in the four-voice chorale style. Notice in particular the chords marked (1), (2), and (3).

FIGURE 19.15 *Dissonances in Four-voice Chorale Style.*

Bach, *Nun danket alle Gott (Now Thank We All Our God)*

1. The seventh chord, D F♯ A C, is in first inversion since the third of the chord (F♯) is the lowest tone.
2. When the apparent seventh (here, C in the bass) appears on a weak part of a beat, it is usually considered a nonharmonic tone. This use is common. This "seventh" is often called a "passing seventh."
3. The seventh chord, D F♯ A C, in root position is temporarily obscured by nonharmonic tones on the first beat of the measure, but its construction becomes clear when the nonharmonic tones resolve to F♯ and C on the second beat.

EXERCISES
19.9, 19.10

In the previous music examples we have identified chords by their spellings. More useful is the identification of a chord by its relationship to a key.

Chords in a Major Key

Any triad in a key can conveniently be identified by the scale step number of its root, using roman numerals, or by the scale step name of its root. A triad built on the fifth (dominant) scale step, for example, can be called a "V triad" (spoken: "five triad"), or a "dominant triad."[10] The triads of Figure 19.16 are known as *diatonic* triads, that is, triads consisting exclusively of scale degrees. (Chords with tones not in the scale are known as *altered* chords.)

FIGURE 19.16 *Triads in a Major Key.*

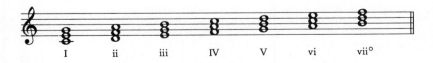

10. Also, V chord ("five chord" or "dominant chord").

The roman numerals may also indicate chord quality:

A large roman numeral (I, IV, V) indicates a major triad.
A small roman numeral (ii, iii, vi) indicates a minor triad.
A small roman numeral with an added ° (vii°) indicates a diminished triad.

The triad number, then, tells us

1. the location of its root in the scale, and
2. the quality of the triad.

For purposes of this text, we will study three commonly used triads, I, IV, and V, and one seventh chord, the V^7.[11] You should be able to spell I, IV, and V easily in all major keys, for example, in B♭ major:

EXERCISES
19.11, 19.12

I: scale step 1 is B♭; the I triad is B♭ D F
IV: scale step 4 is E♭; the IV triad is E♭ G B♭
V: scale step 5 is F; the V triad is F A C

In examining "real" music, we will find the V^7 (dominant seventh) chord used much more frequently than the V triad. As mentioned before, the V^7 is constructed simply by adding a minor third above the fifth of the V triad. This added tone, incidentally, is the fourth scale step of the key.

FIGURE 19.17 *Spelling the V^7 Chord.*

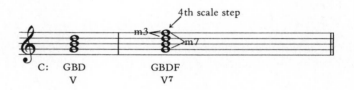

To spell a V^7 chord in E♭ major, for example:

V = B♭ D F

m3 above F = A♭ (or, fourth scale step of E♭ major is A♭)

V^7 = B♭ D F + A♭, or B♭ D F A♭

EXERCISE
19.13

Examples of music may now be analyzed using chord numbers instead of chord spellings. Here are selected measures of music examples presented earlier, this time with roman numeral symbols.

11. In a minor key, i, iv, V, and V^7 are presented in Chapter 21.

FIGURE 19.18   *Use of Roman Numeral Symbols.*

a) from Figure 19. 12, measures 5-8

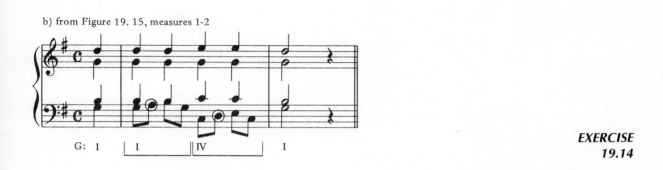

b) from Figure 19. 15, measures 1-2

EXERCISE
19.14

EXERCISE 19.1

Writing triads

Complete each triad by placing two notes on successive lines or spaces above the given note.

(*Return* to page 220)

EXERCISE 19.2

Locating chord members

Place the identification of the chord member, shown above the triad, alongside the appropriate note of the triad.

(*Return* to page 221)

EXERCISE 19.3

Spelling major triads

Spell the major triad built on the tonic note of each of the fifteen major scales.

Key	Scale steps 1, 3, 5			Key	Scale steps 1, 3, 5		
C	C	E	G				
G	G	B	D	F	F	A	C
D	D	F#	A	Bb	Bb	D	F
A	A	C#	E	Eb	Eb	G	Bb
E	E	G#	B	Ab	Ab	C	Eb
B	B	D#	F#	Db	Db	F	Ab
F#	F#	A#	C#	Gb	Gb	B	D
C#	C#	E#	G#	Cb	Cb	Eb	Gb

(*Return* to page 222)

EXERCISE 19.4

Spelling major triads

Spell major triads whose roots are chromatic tones, but not tonic tones listed in Exercise 19.3.

(1)   Root is G♯:   lower G♯ one half step   __G__

                              spell triad on that note   ____ ____ ____

                              raise all notes one half step   ____ ____ ____

(2)   Root is F♭:   raise F♭ one half step   ____

                              spell triad on that note   ____ ____ ____

                              lower all notes one half step   ____ ____ ____

(3)   Root is E♯:   lower E♯ one half step   ____

                              spell triad on that note   ____ ____ ____

                              raise all notes one half step   ____ ____ ____

(4)   Root is A♭♭:   raise A♭♭ one half step   ____

                              spell triad on that note   ____ ____ ____

                              lower all notes one half step   ____ ____ ____

(*Return* to page 222)

EXERCISE 19.5

Spelling major triads

Spell a major triad from a given root and place the triad on the staff. Use any convenient method of spelling.

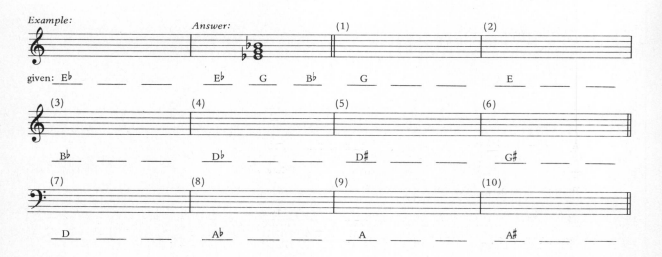

(*Return* to page 223)

232

EXERCISE 19.6

Identifying triads in inversion

A triad in inversion is given. Rearrange the notes on the staff to form a triad in thirds. Spell the triad in thirds, and then indicate first or second inversion for the given triad.

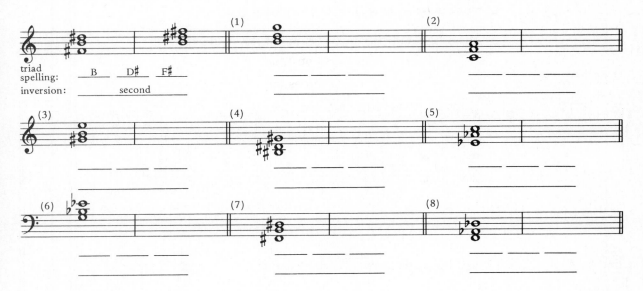

triad spelling: B   D♯   F♯
inversion: second

(*Return* to page *223*)

EXERCISE 19.7

Reducing triads in open position to close position

Rearrange the notes of the given triad so that the position is changed from open to close (the highest note is unchanged). Also, spell the triad in the order of thirds.

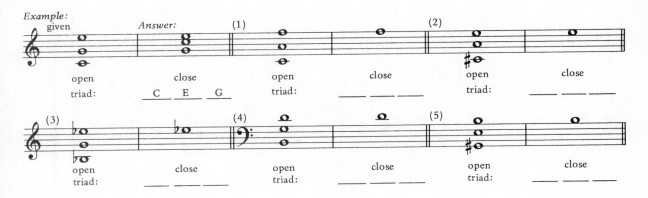

triad: C   E   G

open   close   open   close

triad: _____ _____ _____   triad: _____ _____ _____

(*Return* to page *224*)

EXERCISE 19.8

Locating doubled notes in four-voice triads

Above the staff, write the name of the doubled note.

(*Return* to page *224*)

EXERCISE 19.9

Triads and dissonance

Place spelling of each triad below the staff and circle all tones which are not part of the triad spelling. Chord spellings other than major triads are provided.

(1)   Bach, *Herzlich lieb hab ich dich, O Herr*

* Two nonharmonic tones sound simultaneously. Others will be found in these examples.

234

Bach, *Was Gott tut, das ist wohlgetan*

ACEG

EXERCISE 19.10

Triads, chords, and dissonances

Place the spelling of each chord below the staff. Circle each dissonance, including the seventh of any seventh chord.

(1) **Tempo di Menuetto**

Beethoven, Piano Sonata, Op. 49, No. 2

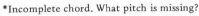

GBD   DF#AC

*Incomplete chord. What pitch is missing?

(2) **Andante**

Gluck, *Orfeo* (1762)

Live with-out my Eu - ri - di - ce? Can I live with-out my love?

235

This well known melody is widely parodied in comedy sketches and in television commercials. It offers a good study in nonharmonic tones and chord analysis. For the latter, it is presented in a key other than the original G major.

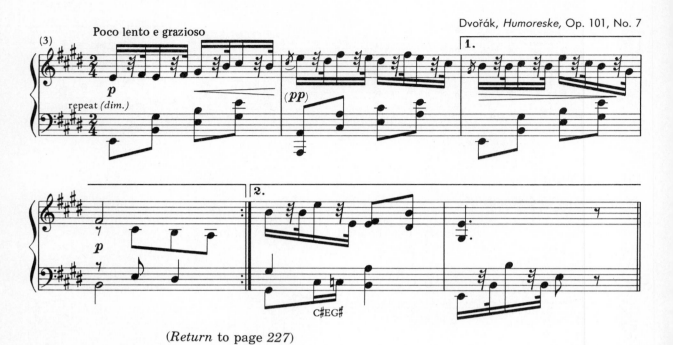

Dvořák, *Humoreske,* Op. 101, No. 7

(*Return* to page 227)

EXERCISE 19.11

Spelling the I, IV, and V Triads

Spell the I, IV, and V triads in the keys indicated.

Key	I			IV			V		
C	C	E	G	F	A	C	G	B	D
D	___	___	___	___	___	___	___	___	___
G	___	___	___	___	___	___	___	___	___
E	___	___	___	___	___	___	___	___	___
F	___	___	___	___	___	___	___	___	___
E♭	___	___	___	___	___	___	___	___	___

EXERCISE 19.12

Spelling the I, IV, and V Triads

Spell the given triad in the key indicated.

NAME _____

<table>
<tr><td>V in the key of C:</td><td>G</td><td>B</td><td>D</td></tr>
<tr><td>IV in the key of B♭:</td><td>____</td><td>____</td><td>____</td></tr>
<tr><td>V in the key of A:</td><td>____</td><td>____</td><td>____</td></tr>
<tr><td>IV in the key of E♭:</td><td>____</td><td>____</td><td>____</td></tr>
<tr><td>I in the key of A♭:</td><td>____</td><td>____</td><td>____</td></tr>
<tr><td>V in the key of E:</td><td>____</td><td>____</td><td>____</td></tr>
<tr><td>IV in the key of F:</td><td>____</td><td>____</td><td>____</td></tr>
</table>

(*Return* to page 228)

EXERCISE 19.13

Spelling V⁷ chords

Spell the V^7 chord when the key is given.

Key	V triad			+	m3 above (or 4th scale step)	=	V^7			
C	G	B	D	+	F	=	G	B	D	F
F	___	___	___	+	___	=	___	___	___	___
A	___	___	___	+	___	=	___	___	___	___
D	___	___	___	+	___	=	___	___	___	___
B♭	___	___	___	+	___	=	___	___	___	___
E	___	___	___	+	___	=	___	___	___	___
A♭	___	___	___	+	___	=	___	___	___	___
E♭	___	___	___	+	___	=	___	___	___	___

(*Return* to page 228)

EXERCISE 19.14

Analysis

Write chord numbers below the staff. Circle each nonharmonic tone and the seventh of each seventh chord. Also, review Exercise 19.10, adding chord numbers.

(1) **Allegro**

(2) **Allegro molto**

(3) **Vivo e risoluto**

Keyboard
Harmony I

Melody Harmonization
Playing the Chord Progression I V^7 I
Procedure for Harmonizing a Melody at the Keyboard
Playing Chord Progressions Using I, IV, and V^7

The completion of our studies of the chords I, IV, and V (V^7) in major keys and of nonharmonic tones leads us to an immediate practical application of this material: *melody harmonization.*

Melody Harmonization

Choosing a series of chords to accompany a given melody is one aspect of the skill of *melody harmonization,* sometimes called "chording." There exists in music literature a virtually countless number of melodies, including large numbers of folk songs, that can be harmonized by I, IV, and V (V^7) only, or even by I and V (V^7) only. In many of these, a satisfactory choice of chords is provided by clues in the melody itself. A familiar folk tune, "Red River Valley," is a good example.

FIGURE 20.1 *Harmonized Folk Melody.*

The clues helping to determine chord choice in this melody, and in most other simple melodies, are:

1. *Notes on the strong beat(s) of the measure.* In measure 1, B on the first beat and G on the third beat suggest G B D, the I triad.
2. *Intervals of a third or larger.* In measure 2, the interval E up to G suggests C E G, the IV triad.

3. *Broken chords.* In measure 3, the notes B-G-B-D are a broken form of G B D.

4. *Long-held notes and repeated notes.* In measure 4, the note A, held for three beats, suggests D F♯ A, the V triad.

5. *Upbeats.* These are usually left unharmonized (indicated in Figure 20.1 by dashes).

With the facility on the keyboard gained from previous work in this text (or from private piano lessons), and with a satisfactory system of chord progression established, could you harmonize this melody at the keyboard? In the simplest way, play the block triad in the left hand at the places indicated, while you sing the tune and/or play the melody with the right hand.

If what you play is placed on staff paper it will look like Figure 20.2.

FIGURE 20.2 *Melody with Block Chord Accompaniment.*

Playing block chords, all in root position, is cumbersome and ordinarily requires visual guiding of the left hand. The chords of Figure 20.2 can also be played without the large leaps through the use of inversions, shown in an easy keyboard formula in Figure 20.3.[1] You can play chords in this manner more or less kinesthetically (by muscular memory), without the distraction at each chord change of having to shift the focus of the eyes from the music down to the keyboard.

FIGURE 20.3 *Formula for Playing I, IV and V⁷ Chords.*

In this formula, V^7 (with the 5th of the chord omitted) is used instead of the V triad because it simplifies the fingering and, at the same time, furnishes a richer sound. This formula can be used for any major key since you already know how to spell a chord from its roman numeral symbol.

1. Neither of these methods of harmonization can produce a professional or artistic performance (as presented in more advanced study), but both are most useful for exploring harmonic patterns and for the achievement of personal pleasure in keyboard activity.

Here is how the complete version of "Red River Valley" looks with the style of chordal accompaniment shown in Figure 20.3, this time in the key of E♭ major, where

$$I = E♭ \quad G \quad B♭$$
$$IV = A♭ \quad C \quad E♭$$
$$V^7 = B♭ \quad D \quad F \quad A♭$$

FIGURE 20.4 *"Red River Valley" in the Key of E♭.*

If, based on experience and skills already developed in chording, you can easily harmonize and play "Red River Valley" and similar melodies, you may skip directly to Exercise 20.5. If you wish to develop this ability, continue with the following study.

Playing the Chord Progression I V⁷ I

The most used chord progression in music is V^7 I. The illustration below includes this progression in a simple arrangement showing the smoothest connections between chords.

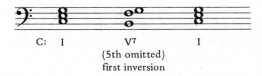

In Figure 20.5 the number before each note indicates the recommended fingering, the thumb being "1" and the little finger "5." Arrows indicate stepwise movement.

FIGURE 20.5 *The Progression I V⁷ I, Left Hand*

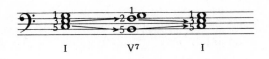

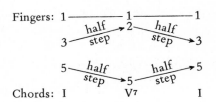

I   V⁷   I

Fingers: 1 ——————— 1 ——————— 1
              half → 2   half
         3 — step   step → 3

         5 — half   half → 5
              step → 5 — step
Chords: I   V⁷   I

In playing the progression I V⁷ I, notice that the thumb repeats the same key while the other fingers each move a half step; the third finger moves up a half step and the fifth finger down a half step in going from I and V⁷, and the reverse when going from V⁷ to I. In the V⁷ chord, the 2nd finger is a whole step below the thumb (applicable to minor as well as major keys).

EXERCISE 20.1

This fingering is applicable to the progression I V⁷ I in any *major key.*

For the application of I and V⁷ in harmonizing a melody at the keyboard, a systematic approach is most effective. The following procedure is recommended.

Procedure for Harmonizing a Melody at the Keyboard

Study:

1. *Key.* Recognize the key of the melody. Spell the I and V⁷ chords (later, when assigned, I IV V⁷) and visualize the notes on lines and spaces of the treble staff. This will help you to determine which melody notes are chord tones.

2. *Chord Choice.* Find clues in the melody (review page 239) that will suggest an appropriate chord choice. Notice any segments of the melody which reappear and will use chords already determined. Write each chord number below the staff and below the note where you will play the chord.

Play:

(If necessary, repeat any step until you can play without hesitation, in tempo.)

1. *Left Hand Alone.* Play the chords you have written.
2. *Right Hand Alone.* Practice the melody.
3. *Hands Together.* Play both melody and chords. Sound a chord on the downbeat of each measure, even though it may be a repeated chord.

For an example, the procedure is applied to the following melody.

FIGURE 20.6 *Melody for Harmonization.*

France

Study:

I   V⁷

1. *Key.* F major. I = FAC; V7 = CEGB♭

2. *Chord Choice.*

Measure 1: the note F is the root (1) of I. CHOOSE THE I CHORD.

Measure 2: G is 5 of V⁷. CHOOSE THE V⁷ CHORD.

Measure 3: on the strong beats of the measure, A and C suggest FAC, I; the interval of the perfect fifth, C down to F is 5 down to 1 of I; the second note of the measure, B♭, must be considered a nonharmonic tone. CHOOSE I.

Measure 4: on the strong beats, E and G are 3 and 5 of V⁷; the interval G down to C is 5 down to 1 of V⁷; the second note of the measure, F, is nonharmonic. CHOOSE V⁷.

Measures 5, 6, 7: these measures are the same as 1, 2, 3.

Measure 8: the interval G down to E is found in the V⁷ chord as 5 down to 3. CHOOSE V⁷ FOR THE FIRST BEAT. The last note, F, is 1 of I. CHOOSE I FOR THE LAST BEAT.

FIGURE 20.7 *Melody with Chord Symbols.*

Play:

(Use Figure 20.7)

1. *Left Hand Alone.* Play the series of chords.
2. *Right Hand Alone.* Practice the melody.
3. *Hands Together.* Play both melody and chords.

You have now completed the procedure for harmonizing a melody at the keyboard. Compare your finished performance with the written-out version on the next page.

FIGURE 20.8 *Melody with Chordal Accompaniment.*

F: I V⁷ I V⁷ I V⁷ I V⁷ I

*When the lowest note of the melody coincides as a unison with the highest note of the left hand chord, the left hand thumb should release this key momentarlly, allowing the right hand to continue with the melody.

In other cases, if the melody overlaps the left hand chord tones, the left hand should play the progression an octave lower (or, less preferred, the right hand could play the melody an octave higher). Advanced study of inversions, beyond the scope of this book, would enable the performer to choose from a variety of positions for the left hand.

EXERCISE 20.2

An added dimension of chording will be found in the use of the IV chord in combination with I and V⁷.

Playing Chord Progressions Using I, IV, and V⁷

Playing the Progression I IV I. Of all the possible progressions using the chords I, IV, and V⁷, the progression I IV I is the easiest to play. The illustration below shows the smoothest connections between chords.

C: I IV I
second
inversion

In Figure 20.9, fingerings are shown before each chord. As before, arrows indicate stepwise (whole or half step) movement.

FIGURE 20.9 *The Progression I IV I, Left Hand.*

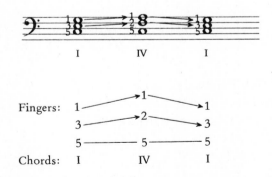

I IV I

Fingers: 1 → 1 → 1
          3 → 2 → 3
          5 — 5 — 5
Chords: I   IV   I

EXERCISE 20.3

In playing the progression, notice that the little finger repeats the same key; in the IV chord, the thumb and 2nd finger form the interval of a major third.

Playing the Progression I IV V⁷ I, Left Hand. The remaining chord connection to be studied occurs in the progression IV V⁷.[2]

FIGURE 20.10 *The Progression I IV V⁷ I, Left Hand.*

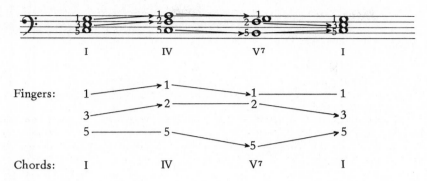

In playing the chords IV V⁷, notice that the 2nd finger repeats the same key while the thumb and 5th finger move stepwise.

EXERCISES
20.4, 20.5

2. The reverse of the IV V⁷ progression, V⁷ to IV (sometimes called *retrogression* as opposed to *progression*), will not be studied in this text. Though commonly used in popular "rhythm and blues," the progression V⁷ IV is uncommon in composed music and traditional folk music.

EXERCISE 20.1

Playing the progression I V⁷ I (left hand)

a) Play the written progressions. Use recommended fingerings for all keys.
Repeat until you can play without hesitation.

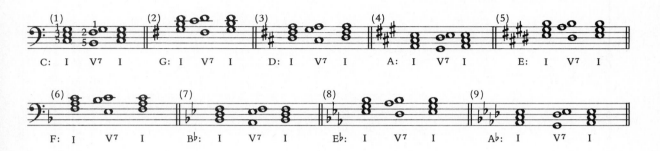

b) Without looking at the music, play I V⁷ I in these keys: (1) C; (2) G; (3) D;
(4) A; (5) E; (6) F; (7) B♭; (8) E♭; (9) A♭.

(To extend this exercise, practice the progression in the remaining keys: B;
F♯; C♯; D♭; G♭; C♭.)

(*Return* to page *242*)

EXERCISE 20.2

Harmonizing melodies using I and V⁷ only

Harmonize each of the following melodies. Use the procedure outlined on
pages 242-43.

*Use the same chord throughout the bracket.

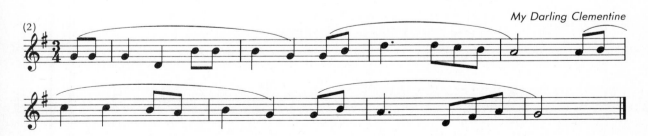

For additional practice, use these melodies from *Music for Sight Singing*, third edition: 70, 72, 83, 84, 85, 101, 103, 168, 187, 227, 228, 244, 246.

(*Return* to page *244*)

EXERCISE 20.3

Playing the progression I IV I (left hand)

a) Play the written progressions. Use recommended fingerings for all keys. Repeat until you can play without hesitation.

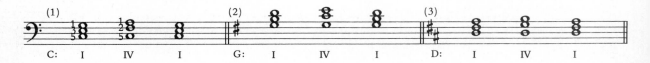

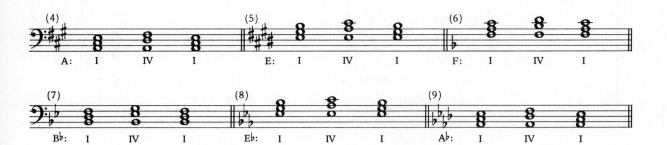

b) Without looking at the music, play I IV I in these keys: (1) C; (2) G; (3) D; (4) A; (5) E; (6) F; (7) B♭; (8) E♭; (9) A. (To extend this exercise, practice the progression in the remaining keys: B; F♯; C♯; D♭; G♭; C♭.)

(*Return* to page 245)

EXERCISE 20.4

Playing the progression I IV V⁷ I (left hand)

a) Play the written progressions. Use recommended fingerings for all keys. Repeat until you can play without hesitation.

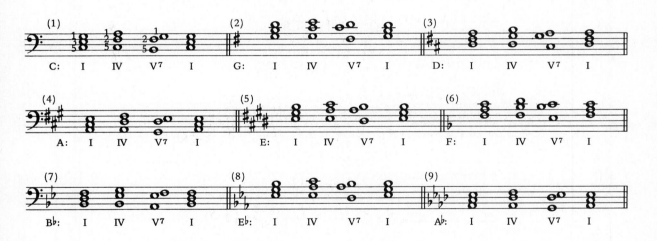

b) Without looking at the music, play I IV V⁷ I in these keys: (1) C; (2) G; (3) D; (4) A; (5) E; (6) F; (7) B♭; (8) E♭; (9) A♭.

(To extend this exercise, practice the progression in the remaining keys: B; F♯; C♯; D♭; G♭; C♭.)

EXERCISE 20.5

Harmonizing melodies using I, IV, and V⁷

Harmonize each of the following melodies at the keyboard. Use the procedures outlined on pages 242-43.

For additional practice, use these melodies in *Music for Sight Singing*, third edition: 170, 183, 225, 230, 265, 319, 337, 339, 354.

CHAPTER TWENTY-ONE

Harmony II:
The Minor, Diminished,
and Augmented Triads

The Minor Triad
Chords in a Minor Key
The Diminished and Augmented Triads

The Minor Triad

The minor triad consists of a minor third and a major third, with the order of the thirds above the root reversed as compared to the major triad, while the interval of the fifth is the same in both.

FIGURE 21.1 *Major and Minor Triads Compared.*

a) Major triad b) Minor triad
M3 + m3   m3 + M3
M3 and P5   m3 and P5

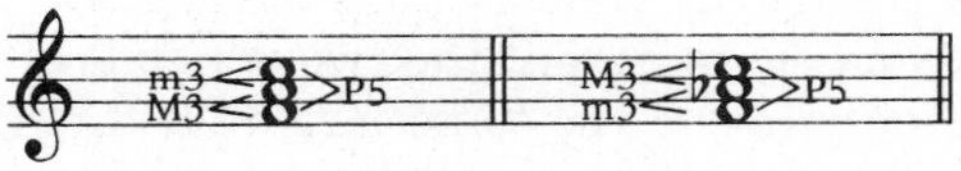

Spelling the minor triad can be accomplished in several ways:

1. If the spelling for a major triad above a given root is known, simply lower the third of that triad by one half step, as in Figure 21.1, F A C to F A♭ C.

EXERCISE 21.1

2. As with major triads, fifteen minor triads can be spelled by selecting steps 1, 3, and 5 of each minor scale, for example:

Minor key	Scale steps 1, 3, 5		
A	A	C	E
F♯	F♯	A	C♯
C	C	E♭	G
B♭	B♭	D♭	F

EXERCISE 21.2

3. Uncommon spellings on the chromatic roots can be spelled in the same manner as those in major (review page 222).

    Problem: Spell a minor triad on E♯
    Solution: Spell a minor triad on E: E G B
                     Raise each note one half step: E♯ G♯ B♯

    Problem: Spell a minor triad on G♭

EXERCISE 21.3

    Solution: Spell a minor triad on G: G B♭ D
                     Lower each note one half step: G♭ B♭♭ D♭

EXERCISE 21.4

4. Spell the minor triad by interval, as shown in Figure 21.1*b*.

There are other respects in which features ascribed to the major triad also apply to the minor triad: triad inversion (review page 223), triad position (review page 224), triad doubling (review pages 224-25), and use of dissonance in conjunction with the triad (review pages 225-27). A new consideration arises when using *chords in a minor key.*

Chords in a Minor Key

Although the system of numbering chords in a minor key follows the same principles used in major keys, there are differences:

1. The quality of a triad on a given scale step in minor will differ from that on the same scale step in major, for example, in C major, I = C E G while in C minor, i = C E♭ G.
2. The melodic form of the scale provides two different versions of both the sixth and seventh scale steps, therefore, each triad containing a sixth or seventh scale step will be found in two forms. For example, in C minor, a triad built on the fourth scale step can be either F A♭ C (iv) or F A♮ C (IV), since A♭ and A♮ represent the two versions of the sixth scale step. Actually it is only above the tonic note that a single diatonic triad is available;[1] any triad other than that built on the tonic includes a sixth or seventh scale step. Observe that those chords using the raised sixth or the raised seventh scale steps are still considered diatonic, rather than altered, since these two raised tones belong to the melodic form of the scale.

We will work in detail only with the tonic (i) triad, the minor iv triad (lowered sixth scale step), the major V triad (raised seventh scale step), and the V^7 chord, as these are commonly used chords.[2] Coincidentally, the chord tones of i, iv, V, and V^7 are diatonic with the harmonic form of the scale. Note also that V and V^7 are spelled identically in parallel major and minor keys.

1. The *final* tonic triad is sometimes found as a major triad, especially in music written before c.1750. The third is often called a "Picardy third." The source of the name is unknown. See Exercise 21.7, example (3).
2. The remaining triads, with examples in C minor are: ii°, D F A♭ and ii, D F A; III, E♭ G B♭ and III +, E♭ G B (an augmented triad); v, G B♭ D; VI, A♭ C E♭ and vi°, A C E♭; VII, B♭ D F and vii°, B D F.

FIGURE 21.2 *Chords in a Minor Key.*

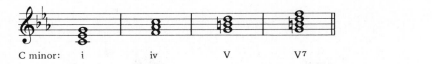

C minor: i   iv   V   V⁷

**EXERCISES
21.5, 21.6,
21.7**

The Diminished and Augmented Triads

Compared with major and minor triads, the use of the diminished triad is infrequent, while the use of the augmented triad could almost be considered rare. Here are the distinguishing features of these triads.

The Diminished Triad

1. The triad is composed of two minor thirds. The interval from its root up to its fifth is a diminished fifth (dim.5). See Figure 21.3a.
2. The triad is used almost exclusively in first inversion. In this inversion, the interval from the fifth of the triad up to its root is an augmented fourth (aug.4). See Figure 21.3b.
3. The symbol for a diminished triad is a small roman numeral with an added °, as in vii°. Used as a diatonic triad, the diminished triad is found on the leading tone in both major and minor keys (vii°) and on the supertonic tone in minor keys (ii°). See Figure 21.3c.
4. The intervals of the diminished fifth and its inversion, the augmented fourth, equally divide the octave. Each interval includes the equivalent of three whole steps, which is why both intervals are known as a *tritone*. See Figure 21.4.

FIGURE 21.3 *The Diminished Triad.*

FIGURE 21.4 *The Tritone.*

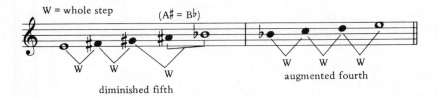

Figure 21.5 shows the use of the two diminished triads in a minor key.

FIGURE 21.5 *vii° and ii° in a Minor Key.*

Bach, *Wo soll ich fliehen hin*

F♯AC
vii°

ACE♭
ii°

The Augmented Triad

1. The triad is composed of two major thirds. The interval from its root up to its fifth is an augmented fifth. See Figure 21.6a.

2. The triad is used in root position and in first inversion. In first inversion, the interval from its fifth up to its root is a diminished fourth. See Figure 21.6a and b.

3. The symbol for an augmented triad is a large roman numeral with an added +, as in I+. It exists as a diatonic triad only on the third degree of a minor scale as III+ (C minor, E♭ G B). See Figure 21.6c. In a major key it is always an altered chord, such as C E G♯ or F A C♯ in C major. See Figure 21.6a.

FIGURE 21.6 *The Augmented Triad.*

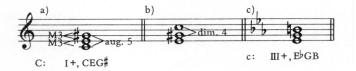

Figure 21.7 shows an augmented triad used as V+, an altered chord in a major key. The original key of this excerpt is C♯ major, where V+ = G♯ B♯ D✕.

FIGURE 21.7 *V+ in a Major Key.*

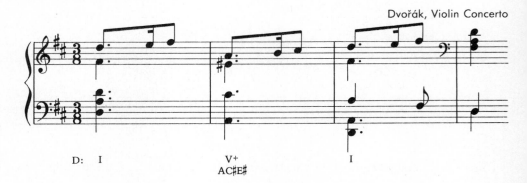

Dvořák, Violin Concerto

D: I

V+
AC♯E♯

I

**EXERCISES
21.8, 21.9**

254

EXERCISE 21.1

Spelling minor triads

Major triads are shown on the staff. After each, write a minor triad by lowering the third of the major triad one half step. Spell each major and minor triad below the staff.

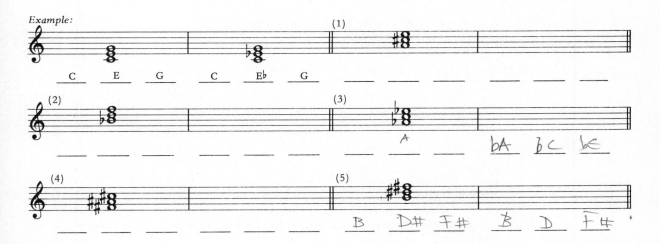

(*Return* to page 251)

EXERCISE 21.2

Spelling minor triads

Spell the minor triad built on each of the tonic notes of the fifteen minor scales.

Minor key	Scale steps 1, 3, 5			Minor key	Scale steps 1, 3, 5		
A	A	C	E				
E	E	G	B	D	D	F	A
B	B	D	F#	G	G	Bb	D
F#	F#	A	C#	C		Eb	G
C#	C#	E	G#	F			
G#	G#	B	D#	Bb			
D#	D#	F#	A#	Eb			
A#	A#	C#	C#	Ab			

(*Return* to page 252)

EXERCISE 21.3

Spelling minor triads

Spell less common minor triads built on chromatic notes.

1. Root is B♯: lower B♯ one half step _____

    spell minor triad on that note _____ _____ _____

    raise all notes one half step _____ _____ _____

2. Root is F♭: raise F♭ one half step _____

    spell minor triad on that note _____ _____ _____

    lower all notes one half step _____ _____ _____

(*Return* to page 252)

EXERCISE 21.4

Spelling minor triads

Spell a minor triad from each of the given roots. Use any convenient method of spelling. Place the triad on the staff.

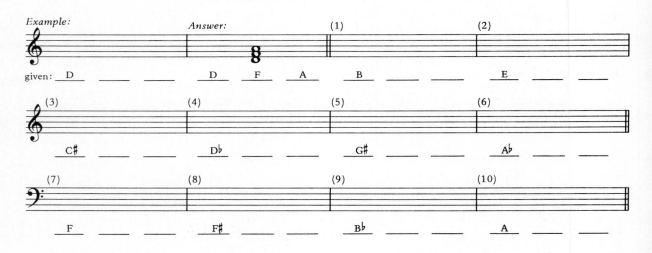

(*Return* to page 252)

EXERCISE 21.5

Spelling minor triads in a key

Spell the i, iv, V, and V⁷ chords in minor keys.

Key	i			iv			V			V⁷			
A	A	C	E	D	F	A	E	G♯	B	E	G♯	B	D
D	__	__	__	__	__	__	__	__	__	__	__	__	__
E	__	__	__	__	__	__	__	__	__	__	__	__	__
G	__	__	__	__	__	__	__	__	__	__	__	__	__
B	__	__	__	__	__	__	__	__	__	__	__	__	__
F♯	__	__	__	__	__	__	__	__	__	__	__	__	__
C	__	__	__	__	__	__	__	__	__	__	__	__	__
F	__	__	__	__	__	__	__	__	__	__	__	__	__

EXERCISE 21.6

Placing the i, iv, V, and V⁷ chords on the staff

The key name is given. Place its signature on the staff and then place the indicated triads on the staff. Be sure to place the appropriate accidental, ♯ or ♮, before the third of the V and V⁷ chords.

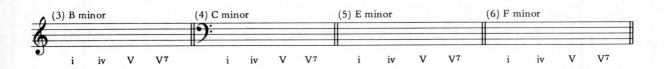

EXERCISE 21.7

Harmonic analysis

Place chord numbers below the staff as appropriate. Circle nonharmonic tones and the sevenths of seventh chords (a few have been circled for you).

Verdi, *La forza del déstino*

(1) Andante

All your threats and proud de - fy - ing, to the winds un - heard are fly - ing, show me pi - ty and for - give, bro-ther, pi - ty and for - give.

Schumann, *Album for the Young,* Op. 68 "The Wild Rider" (original Key, A minor)

(2)

Bach, *Christe, du beistand und deiner Kreuzgemeinde*

(3)

*Review footnote 1, page 252.

(*Return* to page *253*)

EXERCISE 21.8

Spelling diminished and augmented triads

a) From the given root, write two successive minor thirds to complete a diminished triad.

b) From the given root, write two successive major thirds to complete an augmented triad. One of the spellings includes both a sharp and a flat.

a) diminished			*b) augmented*		
B	D	F	C	E	G♯
F♯	A	C	A♭	C	E
E	___	___	F	___	___
G♯	___	___	G	___	___
A	___	___	E♭	___	___
D	___	___	B♭	___	___
G	___	___	A	___	___
C♯	___	___	D♭	___	___

EXERCISE 21.9

Harmonic analysis

Each of these music excerpts contains one example (except as noted) of either a diminished or an augmented triad. Circle the triad, write "dim." for diminished or "aug." for augmented above the triad, and write the triad spelling below the staff.

(1) *Good King Wenceslas*

(2) **Munter** Schumann, *Myrthen*, Op. 25 "Sitz' ich allein"

(4) Look for two triads, one of which is diminished and one is augmented.

Bach, *O Ewigkeit, du Donnerwort*

CHAPTER TWENTY-TWO

Keyboard Harmony II

Playing the Chord Progression i V⁷ i
Harmonizing Melodies in Minor Keys
Playing Chord Progressions Using i, iv, and V⁷

This chapter is devoted to melody harmonization in minor keys using i, iv, and V^7. With the completion of Chapter 21, you have studied the spelling, notation, and analysis of these chords.

Is your keyboard skill sufficient for application of this harmonic material? Or, do you need drill to develop this ability in the hands? Test yourself by chording the following melody. Brahms used only i, iv, and V^7 in his harmonization of this folk melody.

FIGURE 22.1 *Melody for Keyboard Harmonization.*

Brahms, Hungarian Dance No. 4 (original key, F♯ minor)

Compare your results with Figure 22.2 which shows written-out chords in the left hand in a minimal, yet adequate and functional version.

FIGURE 22.2 *Harmonized Melody*.

C minor: i   iv   V⁷   i

iv   i   V⁷   i

If your performance of Figure 22.1 compared favorably with Figure 22.2 and you are confident of your ability to harmonize similar melodies, skip directly to Exercise 22.5. Otherwise, continue with the following study.

Playing the Chord Progression i V⁷ i

Playing the progression i V⁷ i is made easy by the finger control you have developed as a result of playing chords in major keys. A few observations are sufficient to insure correct playing in any minor key.

In this progression, shown in Figure 22.3, notice that the thumb repeats the same key; the little finger moves a half step from tonic to leading tone; and in the V⁷ chord the 2nd finger is a whole step below the thumb. These points of reference are exactly the same for both major and minor keys, the only difference in the progression being in the tonic chord, either major (I) or minor (i).

FIGURE 22.3 *The Progression i V⁷ i, Left Hand.*

C minor: i   V⁷   i

Harmonizing Melodies in Minor Keys

Having practiced the keyboard progression i V⁷ i, we can now apply these chords in a musical way. Refer to p. 242, *Procedure for Harmonizing a Melody at the Keyboard.* With the substitution of minor tonic for major, follow all procedures for *Study-Play* to harmonize melodies in minor keys.

Playing Chord Progressions Using i, iv, and V⁷

Playing the Progression i iv i. In playing this progression, shown in Figure 22.4, notice that the little finger repeats the same key; in the iv chord, the thumb and 2nd finger form the interval of a minor third.

FIGURE 22.4 *The Progression i iv i, Left Hand.*

EXERCISE 22.3

Playing the Progression i iv V⁷ i, Left Hand. When playing iv V⁷ in this progression, shown in Figure 22.5, notice that the 2nd finger repeats the same key while the thumb and 5th finger move stepwise.

FIGURE 22.5 *The Progression i iv V⁷ i, Left Hand.*

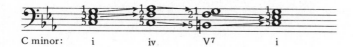

EXERCISES 22.4, 22.5

EXERCISE 22.1

Playing the Progression i V⁷ i (left hand)

a) Play the written progressions. Use recommended fingerings for all keys. Repeat until you can play without hesitation.

b) Without looking at the music, play i V⁷ i in these keys: (1) A minor; (2) E minor; (3) B minor; (4) F♯ minor; (5) C♯ minor; (6) D minor; (7) G minor; (8) C minor; (9) F minor. (To extend this exercise, practice the progression in the remaining keys: G♯ minor; D♯ minor; A♯ minor; B♭ minor; E♭ minor; A♭ minor.)

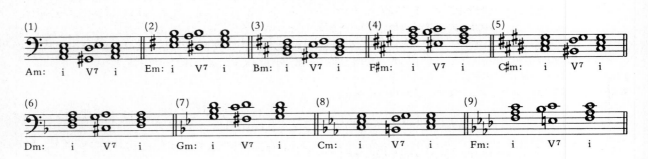

(*Return* to page *262*)

EXERCISE 22.2

Harmonizing melodies using i and V⁷ only

Harmonize each of the following melodies. Use the procedure outlined on pages 242-43.

(*Return* to page 262)

EXERCISE 22.3

Playing the progression i iv i (left hand)

a) Play the written progressions. Use recommended fingerings for all keys. Repeat until you can play without hesitation.

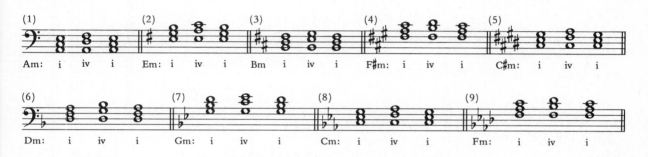

b) Without looking at the music, play i iv i in these keys: (1) A minor; (2) E minor; (3) B minor; (4) F♯ minor; (5) C♯ minor; (6) D minor; (7) G minor; (8) C minor; (9) F minor. (To extend this exercise, practice the progression in the remaining keys: G♯ minor; D♯ minor; A♯ minor; B♭ minor; E♭ minor; A♭ minor.)

(*Return* to page 263)

EXERCISE 22.4

Playing the Progression i iv V⁷ i (left hand)

a) Play the written progressions. Use recommended fingerings for all keys. Repeat until you can play without hesitation.

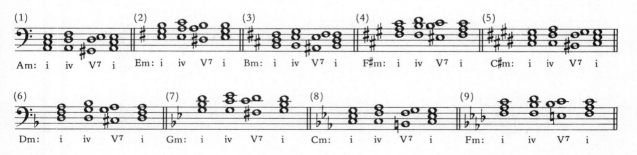

b) Without looking at the music, play i iv V⁷ i in these keys: (1) A minor; (2) E minor; (3) B minor; (4) F♯ minor; (5) C♯ minor; (6) D minor; (7) G minor; (8) C minor; (9) F minor. (To extend this exercise, practice the progression in the remaining keys: G♯ minor; D♯ minor; A♯ minor; B♭ minor; E♭ minor; A♭ minor.)

EXERCISE 22.5

Harmonizing melodies using i, iv, and V⁷

Harmonize the following melodies at the keyboard. Use the procedures outlined on pages 242-43. Include at least one iv chord in each harmonization.

Elementary Acoustics

Hearing is one of the five senses—the others are sight, touch, smell, and taste—through which the body receives stimuli from outside sources. What a person hears is the result of a three-stage process in which (1) an object is set in vibration, (2) the vibrations are conducted through a medium such as air, and (3) the vibrations are received by the ear and transmitted to the brain, which perceives them as sound.

A musical sound combines four qualities which differentiate it from other sounds:

1. *Pitch,* the highness or lowness of a sound
2. *Intensity,* the loudness or softness of a sound
3. *Timbre,* the tone color of a sound, the factor which enables us to distinguish the characteristic sound of a particular instrument or voice (a violin, trumpet, bassoon, a bass singer, etc.)
4. *Duration,* the length of time a sound exists.

The study of both the production of sound and the qualities of sound is known as *acoustics.*[1]

Creating Sound (Vibrations)

To create *vibrations,* an object must be set in motion. There are many ways in music: for example, striking a drum head, blowing on a reed, or drawing a bow across a string. A vibration is the back-and-forth movement of the object so stimulated. Vibrations are usually measured in terms of their *frequency,* that is, the number of back-and-forth movements per second. Frequencies may range from less than one (but more than zero) to many tens of thousands per second.

The vibrations of the original object and of the surrounding air when counted are expressed in terms of *cycles per second* (abbreviated *cps* or Hz[2]). The derivation of this term is not easy to describe in words, but can be seen clearly in a simple demonstration.

---

1. Of the four qualities of sound, duration alone does not depend upon acoustical phenomena.
2. In honor of Heinrich Hertz, 1857–1894, discoverer of radio waves. The abbreviation "Hz" is now more commonly used.

1. Take a blank sheet of paper. On it draw a straight line, the length of the long direction.

FIGURE A1.1 *Demonstrating Vibrations, Step 1.*

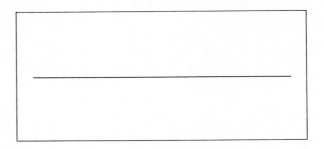

2. Place a pencil point on the left edge of the line. Then move the pencil vertically above the line about 1 or 2 inches, returning along the same mark and continuing below the line for the same distance. Trace back and forth several times. This represents the vibrating body, or vibrating air. You will have made only a straight mark perpendicular to the original line.

FIGURE A1.2 *Demonstrating Vibrations, Step 2.*

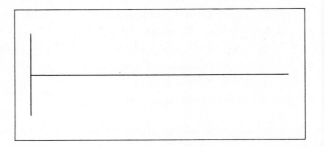

3. Now with your left hand (or if possible, have another person do this) grasp the left side of the sheet of paper and pull it slowly to the left while repeating the up and down action of the pencil. You should get a picture something like this:

FIGURE A1.3 *Demonstrating Vibrations, Step 3.*

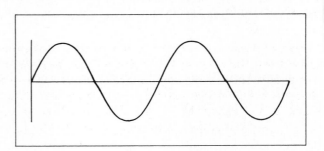

4. In the last diagram, the original straight line represents time (how long it took to pull the paper), while each complete curve (once above the line and once below and returning to the line) is called a *cycle*. Knowing the amount of time and counting the cycles in this time period will tell you the cycles per second. In our illustration if you took one second to pull the paper you would have two cycles per second (2 Hz).

FIGURE A1.4 *Demonstrating Vibrations, Step 4.*

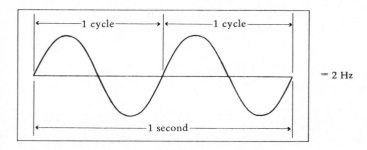

(2 Hz cannot, of course, be heard. Can you visualize a picture for the highest note on the piano, 4,000 Hz?)

Once established, the created vibrations are only vibrations, and not sound, until passage through a medium and transmission to the brain is accomplished. Thus, if there is a lack of a transmitting medium (a vacuum), there is no sound. Or, if the ear does not pick up the vibrations (because of the weakness of the vibrations or a physical defect in the ear), there is—for that person—no sound.

Pitch

The *pitch* of a sound is specifically related to the frequency of vibrations. The higher the frequency, the higher will be the perceived pitch, while the lower the frequency, the lower will be the perceived pitch. Thus, for example, 3,000 Hz will sound much higher than 1,000 Hz. The human ear responds to frequencies in the approximate range of 16-20,000 Hz. The piano produces a range of approximately 28-4,000 Hz, from its lowest to its highest tone.

The Relation of Intervals to Frequency

An interval can be expressed in terms of the numerical ratio between its two tones. For the octave, the ratio is 1:2, meaning that the upper tone of the octave will have double the number of vibrations of the lower tone. If the lower tone is 600 Hz, its octave will be 1200 Hz. For the perfect fifth, the ratio is 2:3. If the lower note of the perfect fifth is 200 Hz, the upper note will be 300 Hz. Similarly, the simplest ratios describe other intervals commonly used in music composition.

FIGURE A1.5   *Ratios of Simple Intervals.*

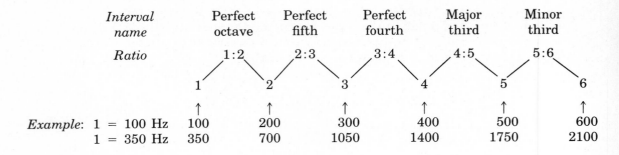

	Perfect octave	Perfect fifth	Perfect fourth	Major third	Minor third

Interval name

Ratio   1:2   2:3   3:4   4:5   5:6

1   2   3   4   5   6

Example: 1 = 100 Hz   100   200   300   400   500   600
          1 = 350 Hz   350   700   1050   1400   1750   2100

The Overtone Series

The series of ratios in Figure A1.5 is coincidental with another phenomenon in sound, the *overtone series*. Simply stated, when any pitch is sounded, a series of higher frequencies that is also created vibrates simultaneously. These higher frequencies, usually inaudible, display the same ratios as those in Figure A1.5, as well as an indefinite series beyond these. Figure A1.6 shows the first sixteen members of an overtone series based on a tone of 88 Hz.

FIGURE A1.6   *The Overtone Series.*

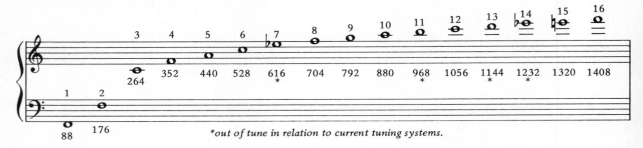

out of tune in relation to current tuning systems.

In addition to the intervals from Figure A1.5, you can see in the overtone series the ratios of these intervals:

major sixth = 3:5   major second = 8:9
minor sixth = 5:8   minor second = 15:16

Members of the overtone series are named in one of two ways; that marked **(1)** is more generally used.

(1)
1 = first partial or fundamental
2 = second partial
3 = third partial
4 = fourth partial

(2)
1 = fundamental
2 = first overtone
3 = second overtone
4 = third overtone

etc.

Pitch Names

Knowing the relationship of pitches does not explain how individual pitches are named. The naming of pitches has always been arbitrary. For example, many different frequencies, including 435, 440, and 446, have in the past been called the tuning A (the A above middle C). Only as recently as 1937 did an international conference assign the name "A" to the frequency of 440 Hz (as used in Figure A1.6), a designation now almost universally used.

Intensity

The *intensity* of a sound, whether it is loud or soft, is determined by the *amplitude* or size of the vibration. The greater the amplitude, the louder, or more intense, the sound will be. In Figure A1.7, both *a* and *b* show 2 Hz. At *a*, the distance traveled above and below the line (the amplitude) is much less than at *b*. Therefore *a* represents a softer sound than *b*. (Understand, of course, that 2 Hz is inaudible at any amplitude, but is convenient for demonstration).

FIGURE A1.7 *Amplitude of Vibrations.*

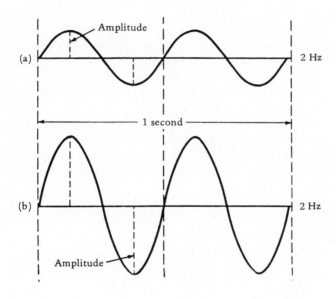

Intensity is measured in units of *decibels* (db. = 1/10 of a *bel*).[3] The greater the amplitude of a sound wave, the higher the db. Musical sounds range from about 25 db. (a soft tone on the violin) to 100db. (the volume of a full orchestra).

Figure A1.8 shows two sounds differing in both pitch and intensity. The pitch at *a* is higher than that at *b* because there are more vibrations per second, but *a* is softer (less intense) than *b* because the vibrations are of a smaller amplitude.

3. The term "bel" is derived from Alexander Graham Bell (1847–1922).

FIGURE A1.8 *Differences in Both Pitch and Intensity.*

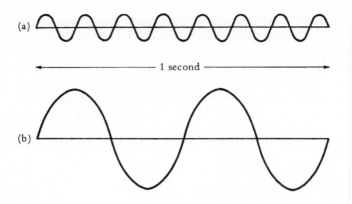

(a)

— 1 second —

(b)

It should be understood that all the preceding diagrams of patterns of vibrations are for demonstration of basic concepts only. A diagram of a real sound is very complex, being a composite of a vibrating rate of the fundamental *and* all its overtones, as well as representing the factor of intensity.

Timbre (tone color)

When you hear two different instruments,[4] say, a violin and a trumpet, play the same pitch, you easily recognize that there is a difference in the sound each produces. The characteristic sound of an instrument is known as its *timbre*. Differences in timbre are related to the differences in the strengths and weaknesses of the partials of a given tone. A given partial for a pitch on one instrument may be more or less intense than the same partial in the pitch produced by the other instrument. In some sounds, some partials may be missing entirely. Figure A1.9 shows two sets of partials (1-6 only), each set representing the same pitch, but each having partials of differing intensities, as reflected by the height of the vertical lines. Because the two pitches so represented differ in the make-up of their partials, one will differ in timbre from the other.

FIGURE A1.9 *Differences in Timbre.*

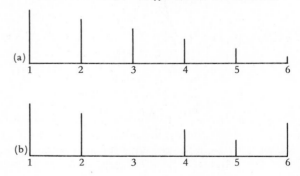

(a)

1   2   3   4   5   6

(b)

1   2   3   4   5   6

Therefore, even if partials are rarely heard as individual sounds, the ear readily picks them up in their various and multiple combinations and thus allows us to hear a great variety of timbres.

4. For purposes of this discussion, the voice is included as an instrument.

Octave Registers
8va
Repeat Signs

Octave Registers

In studying the keyboard you will notice that each letter is used more than once in naming its keys. In fact, there are eight A's, eight B's, and eight C's, plus seven each of the remaining letters of the musical alphabet. Therefore there is a need for a system whereby any one pitch can be designated distinctly from any other pitch of the same letter name. The solution is a system called *octave registers,*[1] whereby the entire range of pitches on the keyboard is divided into octaves, each with its own distinguishing identification. The complete system is shown as Figure A2.1.

Here is how the system works:

General Principle

1. Each *c* is given a designation different from any other *c*.
2. All letter names immediately above a given *c* and up to the next *c* are designated in a manner similar to the given *c*.

Pitches Middle c and Above[2]

3. Middle *c* is designated c^1, called "one-line c," or "c-one."
4. Working up from c^1 (middle *c*), each successive *c* is designated:

c^2	two-line c	c-two
c^3	three-line c	c-three
c^4	four-line c	c-four
c^5	five-line c	c-five

---

1. The word *register* in music ordinarily means range, compass, or placement of pitches.

2. The word *line* as used in item 3 below has nothing to do with the lines of the staff. Rather, *line* should be thought of in the sense of a division, limitation, or boundary. Some theorists use, instead of superscript numerals, simply a vertical line following the letter. Instead of c^1 or c^2, such would appear c′ or c″ and therefore coincide with the terminology one-line c or two-line c.

5. All pitches above c^1 but below c^2 are designated as one-line, such as d^1, e^1, f^1.
   All pitches above c^2 but below c^3 are designated as two-line, such as d^2, e^2, f^2.
   This process applies in a similar manner to pitches above c^3 and c^4. c^5 is the highest pitch on the piano.

Pitches Below Middle c

6. Working down from middle c, each successive c is designated.

c	small c
C	great c
CC	contra c

7. As before, any pitch is designated the same as the nearest c below it.

8. The lowest remaining pitches below CC are located in the *sub-contra* range. The lowest pitch on the piano is AAA, "sub-contra a."

FIGURE A2.1 *Octave Registers,* From Raymond Elliott, *Fundamentals of Music,* 3rd edition © 1971, p. 15. Reprinted by permission of Prentice-Hall, Inc., Englewood Cliffs, New Jersey.

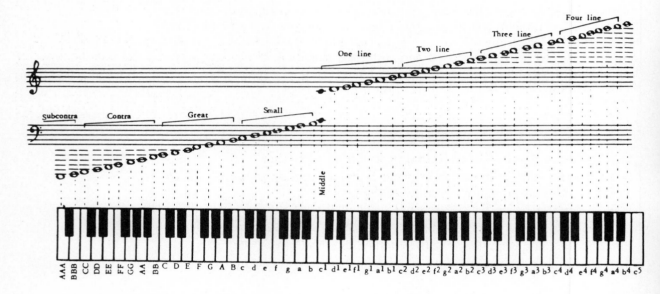

8va

In Figure A2.1, more notes appear above and below the two staves than are actually located on the staff lines and spaces. In fact, of the 52 white notes of the piano keyboard, only 18 appear on the lines and spaces of the treble and bass clefs (five lines and four spaces in each clef). In most music compositions, a very large percentage of pitches can be represented in these two clefs and with one or two ledger lines above or below. On the other hand, there are compositions that utilize many pitches far above or below the staff. Such music containing many ledger lines in the notation can be quite difficult to read. To ease this difficulty, a special sign is used, *8va.*

The sign *8va* or *8,* an abbreviation for the Italian *all' ottava* (at the octave) is used to eliminate the necessity of placing notes many ledger lines above or below the staff, making the music far easier to read. When used above the treble clef, the 8va sign indicates that the notes are to be played one octave higher than written. The notes of Figure A2.2a are written in the location of the pitches c^2, d^2, e^2, f^2, and g^2, over which is placed the sign 8⎤ The passage is performed as though written in the three-line range (c^3, d^3, etc.) as shown in part *b* of Figure A2.2. Observe that the "8" is placed over the first note affected, the dotted line continues to the last note affected, and the sign ends with a vertical line down from the dotted line.

FIGURE A2.2   *8va Above Treble Clef.*

a) written

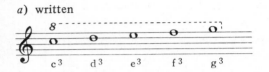

b) played

FIGURE A2.3   *Use of 8va.*

Chopin, Waltz, Op. 64, No. 3

This sign is also used below bass notes to indicate that they are to be performed an octave lower than written. The sign is identical to that used with the treble clef, except that the final vertical line proceeds up from the dotted line: 8⌐

FIGURE A2.4   *8va Below Bass Clef.*

written

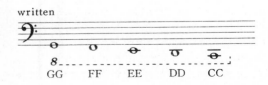

played

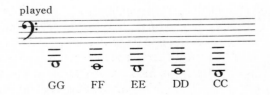

Following the same principle, the 8va sign is sometimes used above the bass clef, but rarely below the treble clef. While the sign is most frequently found in connection with a series of pitches as in the preceding illustrations, 8va may also be used with but a solitary note. An "8" at the last note of a composition may be used without the horizontal line.

Repeat Signs

1. Double Bar and Dots

A repeat sign consists of a double bar preceded by two dots around the third line, and indicates a repetition of the music preceding the sign. Upon reaching the repeat sign the second time, continue on to the next measure.

FIGURE A2.5 *Repeat Sign at End of a Measure.*

When the section to be repeated ends before the end of the measure, the repeat sign (double bar with dots) will be found between the two single bar lines of the measure.

FIGURE A2.6 *Repeat Sign (Double Bar and Dots) Within a Measure.*

If the section to be repeated begins after the beginning of the composition, the section is enclosed by double bars, the first with dots to the right of the double bar and the second with the dots to the left of the double bar.

FIGURE A2.7 *Indication of Repetition of a Section Within a Composition.*

2. First and Second Endings

FIGURE A2.8 *First and Second Endings.*

The first ending (`1.`) indicates a return to the beginning, or to a previous repeat sign (‖:). During the repetition, the music of the first ending is skipped and the piece continues with the second ending (`2.`).

3. D.C., D.S., and Fine

a. Da capo (It. *da capo,* literally, "from the head"), abbreviated D.C., indicates a repeat from the beginning of the composition. See Figure A2.9.

b. Dal segno (It. *dal segno,* "from the sign"), abbreviated D.S., indicates a repeat from the sign 𝄋 . See Figure A2.10.

c. Fine (It. *fine,* "end," pronounced *fee'-nay*) indicates the place where the composition ends after using D.C. or D.S. A double bar is used with the *fine.* See Figures A2.9 and A2.10.

FIGURE A2.9   *The Da Capo.*

FIGURE A2.10   *The Dal Segno.*

APPENDIX 3

The Medieval Modes Other Scale Forms

The structures of both our present day major and natural minor scales are identical to two scales in earlier music history. Eight-note scale systems in Western music evolved as early as the 8th century A.D., and by 1600 music was commonly written in a system of six different scales, called *modes*. These six modes can be found quickly on the piano keyboard by playing up an octave from each note given below (Fig. A3.1), using only white keys. You will observe that each mode consists of five whole steps and two half steps, and that the half steps are always E-F and B-C but each mode differs from the others because of the varying locations of the half steps. These differences, together with the name of each mode, are shown in Figure A3.1.

FIGURE A3.1 *Modes.*

First note	White-key scale														Mode
A	a	2 b	3 c	d	5 e	6 f	g	a							Aeolian
		½			½										
(B)[1]															(Locrian)
C			c	d	3 e	4 f	g	a	7 b	8 c					Ionian
					½				½						
D				d	2 e	3 f	g	a	6 b	7 c	d				Dorian
					½				½						
E					1 e	2 f	g	a	5 b	6 c	d	e			Phrygian
					½				½						
F						f	g	a	4 b	5 c	d	7 e	8 f		Lydian
									½			½			
G							g	a	3 b	4 c	d	6 e	7 f	g	Mixolydian
									½			½			

1. Theoretically, a mode called Locrian can be constructed on B, but it was not used in musical practice.

Ionian and Aeolian: Major and Minor

Through evolutionary processes, the number of scale systems was reduced to two by the mid-seventeenth century. The Ionian mode became the pattern for the major scale. The Aeolian mode was also retained, and became the pattern for the basic minor scale: the pure, or natural form of the minor scale.

The Role of "Musica Ficta" in Scale Development

Of the seven possible modal scales, only two, the Ionian and the Lydian, contain a leading tone. This lack of a leading tone in ascending forms of the other modes was recognized very early in the history of the use of modes. Performers often preferred the sound of leading tone to tonic rather than a whole step, and, in performance of music written with an ascending whole step between 7 and 8, would sometimes raise the seventh scale step to create a leading tone. This practice, part of a system known as *musica ficta* (false music), was condoned by performers and composers alike.[2]

By adding a leading tone, the Mixolydian mode displays the same scale structure as Major:

$$G\ A\ B\ C\ D\ E\ F\sharp\ G$$

the Aeolian the same as Minor, harmonic form:

$$A\ B\ C\ D\ E\ F\ G\sharp\ A$$

and the Dorian the same as Minor, melodic form:

$$D\ E\ F\ G\ A\ B\ C\sharp\ D$$

Figure A3.2 shows a melodic line in the Aeolian mode, with the seventh scale degree G raised to G♯. The sharp *above* the note indicates that it was *not* written by the composer but rather reflects the probable performance based on known principles of *musica ficta*.

FIGURE   A3.2   *Use of Musica Ficta.*

Palestrina (1525-1594), *Missa de Feria*

---

2. This principle was not applied to the Phrygian mode. For more detailed information, consult articles under the heading *musica ficta* in music dictionaries, or in music history books, chapters on Medieval and Renaissance music.

In another practice common to *musica ficta,* B was lowered to B♭ in certain circumstances. When applied to the Lydian mode, the resulting scale structure is the same as major:

F G A B♭ C D E F

When applying both varieties of *musica ficta* (♭6 and ♯7) to the Dorian, the resulting scale structure is the same as minor, harmonic form:

D E F G A B♭ C♯ D

Thus the three forms of the minor scale are simply a result of performance practices applied to modal structures. Even today, the minor key signature is that for the Aeolian mode, while changes in the sixth and seventh scale degrees are placed in the music itself.

Other Scale Forms

1. The *chromatic scale* is a 12-note scale, utilizing half steps only within its octave. The ascending form generally uses sharp signs (♯), while the descending form uses flat signs (♭).

FIGURE A3.3 *The Chromatic Scale.*

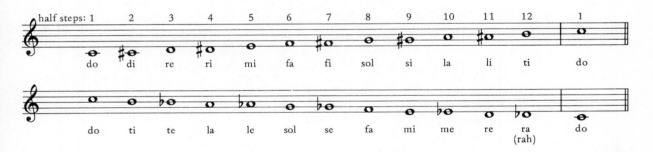

No complete compositions (before the twentieth century) are based on this scale, but, in a melodic line, a series of half steps is often said to be derived from the chromatic scale. In the twentieth century, the *tone row,* a 12-note series using all the tones of the chromatic scale, is often used as a basis for composition rather than the traditional 7-note scale. As originally devised by Arnold Schönberg (1874-1951), the tone row consists of the twelve tones of the chromatic scale, the order chosen arbitrarily. One such row, as devised by Anton Webern (1883-1945) for his Concerto for Nine Instruments, is shown as Figure A3.4. In this particular row, each three-note grouping contains the interval of a minor second and a major third, although each group is in a different melodic configuration.

FIGURE A3.4 *Example of a Tone Row.*

2. The *pentatonic scale* is a 5-note scale, easily found by playing only the black keys on the piano. Its structure, M2, M2, m3, M2, m3, can be found by starting on any note: three possibilities are shown in Figure A3.5, *a, b,* and *c.*

FIGURE A3.5 *The Pentatonic Scale.*

Debussy, *Reflets dans l'eau*

In Figure A3.5*d,* the scale is indicated by the bracket below the bass clef. Four-note segments of the scale can be seen in the treble clef: E♭ D♭ B♭ A♭ in the highest voice, and B♭ A♭ E♭ D♭ in the inner voice.

3. The *whole tone* scale is a 6-note scale using only whole steps. In notation, the scale always includes an interval written as a diminished third, shown in Figure A3.6*a,* such as C♯-E♭ or D♯-F. In the example from Debussy, Figure A3.6*b,* the scale is G A (B) C♭D ♭E♭ F G.

FIGURE A3.6 *The Whole Tone Scale.*

Debussy, *Reflets dans l'eau*

4. *Scale patterns using augmented seconds* (other than between the sixth and seventh scale steps in minor) are frequently found in non-Western cultures, particularly in Eastern Europe,[3] the Near East, and North Africa. Anyone familiar with the melody of Tchaikovsky's *Marche Slav* (Figure A3.7*b*) will recognize its source in the Slovakian folk song (Figure A3.7*a*), where the augmented second occurs between scale steps 3 and 4.

3. A scale with augmented seconds between 3-4 and 6-7 is sometimes known as a *Hungarian scale* or a *Gypsy scale.*

FIGURE A3.7 *Scale with Augmented Second.*

A number of melodies showing various locations of the augmented second can be found in Ottman, *More Music for Sight Singing* (Prentice-Hall, Inc., 1981), including:

Augmented seconds between 2-3 and 6-7; melody 1041 (Lebanon)

Augmented second between scale steps 2-3; melody 1047 (Slovakia)

"Major" scale with augmented second between 4-3 descending only; melody 1049 (Tunisia)

Keyboard Scale Fingerings

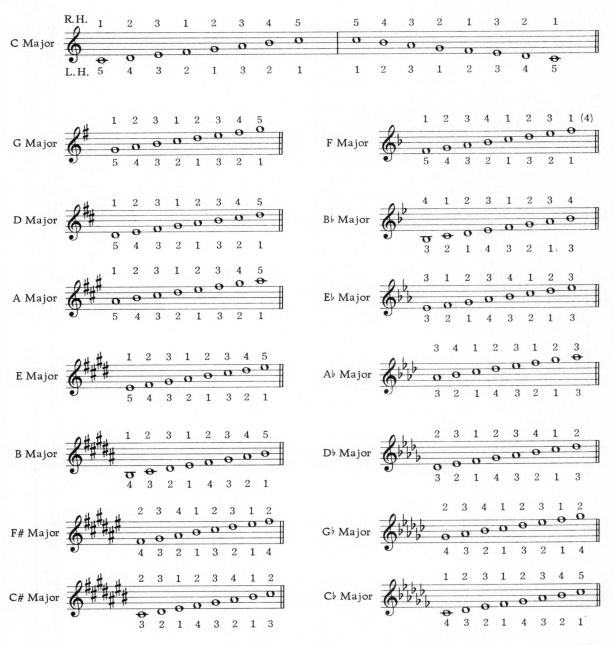

All forms of A Minor use the same fingering.

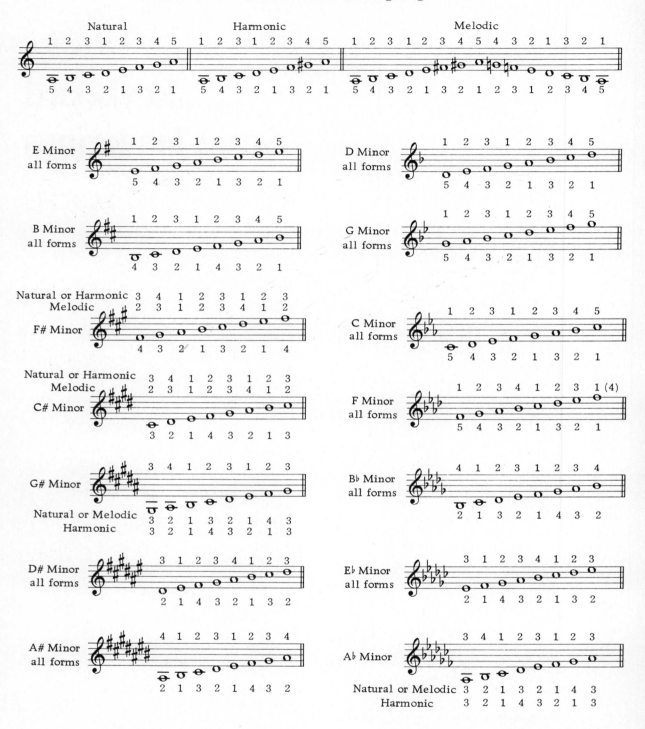

Foreign Words and Musical Terms

Most music commonly performed at the present time contains directions for performance, particularly in reference to tempo and dynamics. These markings were first added to music scores by a few Italian composers in the seventeenth century. As this procedure became more widespread, directions in Italian became standard in all languages. In the late nineteenth century, composers began using terms from their native languages, such as French, German, and English, though the older Italian terms continued to be commonly used.

This list presents a selection of terms frequently encountered in music, including all terms found in *Music for Sight Singing* and *More Music for Sight Singing*. Unless otherwise indicated, the language is Italian (Fr. = French, G. = German, L. = Latin).

A

a, à (Fr.) by
accelerando getting faster
adagietto slightly faster than adagio
adagio slow, leisurely
ad libitum (L.) at will (abbr. *ad lib.*)
affetto emotion, passion
afettuoso very expressively
affretti hurried
agitato agitated
al to
all', alla to the, at the, in the, in the style of
allant (Fr.) stirring, bustling
all'ottava perform an octave higher (when above the notes); perform an octave lower (when below the notes)
all'unisono in unison
allargando growing broader, slowing down with fuller tone (abbr. *allarg.*)

allegretto moderately fast; slower than allegro
allegro lively, fast
amoroso amorous, loving
andante moderately slow
andantino somewhat quicker than andante
animando with growing animation
animato animated
animé (Fr.) animated
a piacere freely
appassionato with passion
assai very
assez (Fr.) enough, rather
a tempo return to the original tempo after a change
attacca begin next section at once
aussi (Fr.) as

B

belebter (G.) lively
ben well
bewegt (G.) moved

bien (Fr.) well, very
brio vivacity, spirit, fire
brioso with fire, spiritedly

C

cantabile in a singing style
coda end of piece
col', coll', colla, colle, with
comodo, commodo comfortable tempo

con with
coulé (Fr.) smoothly
crescendo increasing in volume (abbr. *cresc.*)

D

da capo from the beginning (abbr. *D.C.*)
dal segno from the sign (abbr. *D.S.*)
deciso with decision
declamato in declamatory style
decrescendo decreasing in volume (abbr. *decresc.*)
diminuendo decreasing in volume (abbr. *dim.*)
dolce soft

dolcissimo as soft as possible
dolendo doleful, sad
dolore pain, grief
doloroso sorrowful
doppio double
douce, doux (Fr.) soft, sweet

E

e and
einfach (G.) simple, plain
energico energetic, vigorous
ernst (G.) earnest, serious
erregeter (G.) excited

espressivo expressive (abbr. *espress.*)
et (Fr.) and
etwas (G.) somewhat

F

feierlich (G.) solemn
ferocé (Fr.) wild, fierce
fine end
flebile tearful, plaintive
forlane Italian dance; fast tempo, $\frac{6}{4}$ or $\frac{6}{8}$ meter
forte loud (abbr. *f*)

forte-piano loud, then immediately soft (abbr. *fp*)
fortissimo very loud (abbr. *ff*)
forzando with force (abbr. *fz*)
frisch (G.) glad, joyous
frölich (G.) glad, joyous
fuoco fire

G

gai (F.) gay, brisk
gaiment, gayment (Fr.) gaily, briskly,
gavotte French dance; moderate tempo, quadruple time
gesangvoll (G.) in a singing style
geschwind (G.) swift, rapid
giocoso playful
giojoso joyful, mirthful
gioviale jovial, cheerful

giusto correct
gracieusement (Fr.) graciously
gracieux (Fr.) gracious
grandioso grand, pompous
grave slow, ponderous
grazia grace, elegance
grazioso graceful
gut (G.) good, well
gut zu declamiren (G.) clearly declaimed

H

heimlich (G.) mysterious

herzlich (G.) heartily, affectionate

I

im (G.) in
immer (G.) always
innig (G.) heartfelt, fervent
innigkeit (G.) deep emotion

istesso same
istesso tempo same tempo (after a change of time signature)

J

joyeuse, joyeux (Fr.)   joyous

K

klagend (G.)   mourning

kurz (G.)   short, crisp

L

ländler   Austrian dance; slow, in triple time
langoureuse, langoureux (Fr.)   langourous
langsam (G.)   slow
langsamer (G.)   slower
languido   languid
largamente   broadly
larghetto   not as slow as largo
larghissimo   very slow
largo   slow and broad, stately
lebhaft (G.)   lively, animated
legato   smoothly connected
leger (Fr.)   light

leggiero   light (abbr. *legg.*)
leicht (G.)   light
leise (G.)   soft
lent (Fr.)   slow
lentement (Fr.)   slowly
lenteur (Fr.)   slowness
lento   slow
liberamente   freely
lieblich (G.)   with charm
l'istesso tempo   same as *istesso tempo*
lustig (G.)   merry, lusty

M

ma   but
mächtig (G.)   powerful
maestoso   with majesty or dignity
malinconico   in a melancholy style
marcato   marked, emphatic
marcia   march
marziale   martial
mässig (G.)   moderate
même (Fr.)   same
meno   less
mesto   sad
mezzo   half (mezzo forte, *mf,* mezzo piano, *mp*)
minuet (menuet)   French dance; moderate tempo, triple time

misterioso   mysteriously
mit (G.)   with
moderato   moderately
modéré (Fr.)   moderate
modérément (Fr.)   moderately
molto   much, very
morendo   dying away
mosso   "moved" (*meno mosso,* less rapid; *più mosso,* more rapid)
moto   motion
munter (G.)   lively, animated
mutig (G.)   spirited

N

nicht (G.)   not
niente   nothing
non   not

non tanto   not so much
non troppo   not too much
nobilimente   with nobility

O

ossia   or

ottava   octave

P

parlando   singing in a speaking style
pas (Fr.)   not
pas trop lent (Fr.)   not too slow

pesante   heavy
peu (Fr.)   little
peu à peu (Fr.)   little by little

piano soft (abbr. *p*)
pianissimo very soft (abbr. *pp*)
più more
plus (Fr.) more

poco little
presto fast, rapid
prima, primo first

Q

quasi as if, nearly (as in *andante quasi allegretto*)

R

rallentando slowing down (abbr. *rall.*)
rasch (G.) quick
rhythmique (F.) rhythmic, strongly accented
rigaudon Provençal dance; moderate tempo, quadruple time
rinforzando reinforcing; sudden increase in loudness for a single tone, chord, or passage (abbr. *rfz*)

risoluto strongly marked
ritardando slowing down (abbr. *rit.*)
rubato perform freely
ruhig (G.) quiet

S

sanft (G.) soft
sans (Fr.) without
sarabande Spanish dance; slow tempo, triple time
scherzando playfully
schnell (G.) fast
sec, secco dry
segue follows; next section follows immediately; or, continue in a similar manner
sehr (G.) very
semplice simple
semplicemente simply
sempre always
sentito with feeling
senza without
sforzando forcing; perform a single note or chord with sudden emphasis (abbr. *sfz.*)

siciliano Sicilian dance; moderate tempo, $\frac{6}{8}$ or $\frac{12}{8}$ meter
simile similarly; continue in the same manner (abbr. *sim.*)
slancio impetuousness
sostenuto sustained
sotto under
sotto voce in an undertone; subdued volume
spirito, spiritoso spirit
staccato detached; with distinct breaks between tones
stark (G.) strong
stentando slowing down (abbr. *stent.*)
stringendo pressing onward
subito suddenly

T

tant (Fr.) as much
tanto so much
tempo time
tempo giusto correct tempo
tendrement (Fr.) tenderly
teneramente tenderly
tenuto held
tempo time
tranquillo tranquil

traurig (G.) sad
très (Fr.) very
trio In a minuet or scherzo, the middle section between the minuet (scherzo) and its repetition
triste (It., Fr.) sad
tristement (Fr.) sadly
tristezza sadness, melancholy
trop (Fr.) too much
troppo too much

U

un, uno one, a, an
una corde one string; on the piano: use soft pedal (abbr. *u.c.*)

und (G.) and
unisono unison

V

vif (Fr.) lively
vite (Fr.) quick
vivace very fast

vivamente very fast
vivo lively

W

waltz Austrian-German dance; moderate tempo, triple time

walzer (G.) waltz

Z

zart (G.) tender, delicate
zartlich (G.) tenderly

ziemlich (G.) somewhat, rather
zierlich (G.) delicate, graceful

Index